ISLAMIC CAPITAL MARKETS

AN INTRODUCTORY AND PRACTICAL GUIDE

PUBLISHED BY: Motivate Media Group

DUBAI:
Media One Tower, Dubai Media City
PO Box 2331, Dubai, UAE
Tel: (+971 4) 427 3000
Fax: (+971 4) 428 2268
books@motivate.ae
www.booksarabia.com

ABU DHABI:
Makeen Tower, 9th Street, Al Zahiyah
PO Box 43072, Abu Dhabi, UAE
Tel: (+971 2) 657 3490

RIYADH:
Al Hamad Tower, King Fahad Road
Al Olaya, Riyadh, KSA
Tel: (+966 11) 834 3595

LONDON:
Acre House, 11/15 William Road
London NW1 3ER, UK

DIRECTORS: Obaid Humaid Al Tayer, Ian Fairservice
PUBLISHER: Ian Fairservice
GROUP DIRECTOR: Andrew Wingrove
PUBLISHING MANAGER: Vaarunya Bhalla
SENIOR EDITOR: Aswathy Sathish
ART DIRECTOR: Noel de la Pena

British Library Cataloguing-in-Publication Data.
A catalogue record for this book is available from the British Library.

ISBN: 978 1 86063 556 4
MEDIA REGULATORY OFFICE APPROVAL NUMBER: MC-02-01-7339780

ISLAMIC

CAPITAL MARKETS

AN INTRODUCTORY

AND

PRACTICAL GUIDE

QUDEER LATIF

PREFACE

I HAVE BEEN FORTUNATE to be involved in the development and growth of the Islamic finance industry for nearly two decades. During this journey, I have had the pleasure of working with many talented individuals, teams and organisations across the world. Whilst there are many organisations that are active in spreading knowledge and educating the next generation of Islamic finance practitioners, and there has in recent years been the development of Islamic finance courses, degrees and centres of knowledge and excellence, there still remains much misunderstanding and many misconceptions. I therefore decided to write this practical book to try and open up the world of Islamic capital markets, or sukuk, to as many people as possible, to dispel many misunderstandings that exist and to try and communicate in a practical user-friendly way the processes and key steps for the structuring of sukuk and implementation in the context of the modern global financial systems.

There are a number of legal, commercial and regulatory considerations that need to be taken into account – whilst these are all critical, they are often the same as the considerations that need to be taken into account when structuring, documenting and issuing a conventional bond. The key difference however in what makes a sukuk different from a bond is sharia compliance. In other words, ensuring a sukuk is compatible and aligned with the rulings of Islamic fiqh or jurisprudence as it relates to *fiqh-al-muamalat* (in other words, the Islamic jurisprudence that relates to Islamic commercial and financial matters). There is sometimes an inherent conflict between how certain issues are viewed from a sharia perspective and how they may be viewed from a legal or regulatory perspective, but my aim is to allow readers to understand how these instruments are structured and the processes that are involved and ultimately how regard is given to the fact these are instruments that need to be approved as being sharia compliant.

The question I am often asked is are sukuk really truly sharia-compliant? It is not a question that is easy to answer and indeed not a question that has a binary answer. Whilst compliance with a rule is often viewed as binary (i.e. an instrument is either compliant or not), sharia compliance in the world of financial matters is often one of degree. Every transaction is always unique – there is always a desire to make each new transaction slightly 'better' from a sharia perspective, or put in another way, more sharia compliant. There can be no doubt that the optimum Islamic finance instrument is not a debt-based instrument but rather one that is based on risk sharing and allocation of commensurate rewards. In other words, the greater the risk the greater the reward. But herein lies the fundamental paradigm in the dichotomy of Sukuk and modern financial systems i.e. most sukuk are commercially intended to replicate the economics of a conventional fixed income security.

There are a number of reasons for this – fundamentally investors that purchase sukuk can be either Islamic investors or conventional investors. Islamic investors that buy sukuk will include the treasury department of Islamic banks or financial institutions which are set up and regulated as banks and not private equity houses. They are looking for a long-dated investment with a fixed periodic return and these banks, due to the regulatory environment in which they operate, require a fixed debt-based return rather than a return based on a risk-sharing approach. There are also a large number of conventional investors that will purchase sukuk such as asset managers, pension companies, insurance companies etc and such investors will only do so if the sukuk has the same economic and legal features as a conventional bond.

The beauty of Islamic finance, as readers will learn, is that the primary sources of sharia have set out some basic principles of Islamic finance which are sacrosanct. These are not difficult to comprehend. However, sharia has also given sufficient flexibility within these parameters.

Finally, whilst I am an English-qualified solicitor and a partner in a global law firm and have been fortunate enough to establish and lead the growth of one of the pre-eminent global Islamic finance practices globally, I am not academically qualified in matters of sharia. I have been fortunate enough to have been able to learn directly from some of the leading Islamic finance scholars across the world over the last two decades and this is a journey that continues. This book is not intended to cover the fiqh (or Islamic rationale from a sharia perspective) for certain decisions or positions that are adopted in financial and commercial transactions, but rather is intended to be a wider practical understanding of how these instruments can be made to work in the modern financial world. This book does not constitute sharia, legal or regulatory advice but I hope will serve as a useful reference point for those who wish to learn more.

Before we get into the detail, I would also like to flag that Islamic finance is in a constant evolutionary pattern. That does not mean that sharia itself evolves but rather the application and interpretation of sharia may evolve. There are certain rules which are binary such as the prohibition of interest (or *riba*) but suitably qualified scholars are permitted to interpret Islamic finance jurisprudence in the application of the modern financial instruments. This methodology of evolving interpretation and application through consensus is an accepted and key rule of Islamic finance. The consequence of this is what may have been considered sharia-compliant a few years ago and accepted by the Islamic finance market may no longer be sharia-compliant today, and equally, there will undoubtedly be further developments in the Islamic finance market which are not currently considered acceptable. By way of example, my first sukuk transaction was in 2003 and certain features of that instrument would definitely not be acceptable in today's market from a sharia perspective!

My views therefore set out in this book are applicable as of August 2022.

CONTENTS

CHAPTER 1

ORIGINS AND DEVELOPMENT OF SUKUK

1.1. Origins of Sukuk

Whilst the market for sukuk as a financial instrument is only two decades old, the high-profile growth and prevalence of sukuk in the Islamic finance industry over this period has made the term 'sukuk' synonymous with the Islamic capital markets. This form of sharia-compliant alternative to interest-bearing fixed income securities has led to the product being commonly referred to as 'Islamic bonds'.

The first domestic sukuk as a financial instrument was issued in 1998 in Malaysia and the first global USD-denominated sukuk was issued in 2002.

The market has grown from one that was around USD 1–2 billion per year in its early years to a market that saw issuance worth nearly USD 180 billion in 2021. The total amount of sukuk now outstanding globally is now close to USD 1 trillion. The vast majority of this has been issued in international currencies (predominantly USD) but there are also a large number of domestic sukuk issuances issued in local currencies.

Whilst this book is intended to be a practical understanding of a sukuk, it is worth spending a little time to understand the background and context.

There is evidence to suggest that elementary forms of sukuk structures were used within Muslim societies as early as the Middle Ages in two different forms:

- Commercial paper that represented financial obligations originating from trade. To avoid traders carrying large amounts of money during the trading season, purchasers of goods used to provide 'sak' (which is the singular of sukuk) that represented the owner's right to the money in a safe and secure location. This 'sak' has developed in the modern financial system to become the 'cheque'.

- Certificates that could be exchanged for goods or groceries. It was a method of paying salaries of government officers, who could then redeem such certificates in exchange for actual goods or groceries that the sukuk represented; i.e. similar to the modern 'coupon' system or rationing certificate.

The modern form of the sukuk can be derived from a decision of the Islamic Jurisprudence Council (the IJC) dated 6–11 February 1988 which stated that: "any combination of assets (or the usufruct of such assets) can be represented in the form of written financial instruments which can be sold at a market price provided that the composition of the group of assets represented by the sukuk consist of a majority of tangible assets."

Although the IJC's decision is not binding, the significance of the institution in the Muslim world saw the issuance and trading of Islamic financial instruments which were approved as being sharia-compliant in Malaysia from 1998 onwards. A number of these were based on the sukuk assets being debt – whilst the sale/ transfer of debt is permitted by the Shafi jurisprudence (prevalent in countries like Malaysia and Indonesia), the more conservative schools of thought prevalent in the Gulf Co-operation Council (the GCC) countries had a conceptual concern with the secondary trading of sukuk certificates where the underlying sukuk asset was debt alone.

A standard in May 2003 on 'Investment Sukuk' published by the Accounting and Auditing Organisation for Islamic Financial Institutions (AAOIFI)[1] led to a paradigm shift in sukuk. The standard was backed by 14 prominent Islamic scholars from the Middle East, Malaysia, the Indian sub-continent and Africa and helped create cross-border convergence on sukuk across the four main schools of Islamic jurisprudence. Whilst there has been much development since 2003, this original standard on Investment Sukuk is the foundation of the modern global sukuk market.

1.2. Development of Sukuk

Whilst AAOIFI Standards have been in existence for many years, and the first AAOIFI Standard on sukuk was issued in 2003, there has been much debate on the use of all the standards for many years. This discussion amplified in 2008 and again since 2019.

In 2008 AAOIFI issued clarificatory statements that certain types of sukuk structures could not be used for fixed income securities, or to be more particular, sukuk which used *mudaraba* and/ or *musharka* as the underlying Islamic instrument could not be used in conjunction with a fixed price purchase undertaking. The

---

1   AAOIFI Sharia Standard No. 17.

rationale for this is that a *mudaraba* and musharaka are intended to provide equity risk instruments. Whilst this did not impact sukuk that had already been issued prior to that date, it did mean that any sukuk issued after that date could no longer adopt this approach.

In 2019 the UAE Central Bank (which is the regulator of all banks/financial institutions in the UAE) established a centralised sharia authority referred to as the Higher Sharia Authority (the HSA). This body has mandated that all Islamic banks in the UAE and all financial institutions which provide Islamic finance must adhere to AAOIFI standards in the structuring and execution of sukuk transactions. Whilst there are certain limited exceptions, the rules for determining if an exception may be available and the terms of any such exception are complicated. This is important because there is a large number of Islamic investors based in the UAE and it is a key market for sukuk distribution, so if a sukuk is intended to be structured, arranged or marketed by UAE-based Islamic investors, it must, as a general principle, comply with all AAOIFI standards. Whilst there will inevitably be some 'adjustment' time required for stakeholders, investors and third parties, the change is overall welcome, as in the mid- to long-term, it will: (i) introduce a higher level of sharia compliance into the UAE market; (ii) ultimately lead to a more consistent interpretation and application of sharia; (iii) lead to a greater degree of confidence in the UAE market. At the time of writing, the UAE market is still going through this 'adjustment' phase which inevitably is having an impact on current transactions.

One key standard which is now referred to is the AAOIFI Standard No. 59, which has introduced a number of requirements. Whilst the standard is called '*Bay-al-dayn*', which essentially means 'trading of debt', there are a number of important requirements which impact all sukuk transactions. The key points include:

- A sukuk structured on a *murabaha*-basis only (i.e. *sukuk-al-murabaha*) is no longer permitted. Whilst this is still used for domestic transactions in certain countries such as Malaysia, it is no longer possible to use this as a standalone structure in the UAE.

- A sukuk must have a minimum tangibility of 51 per cent. If the tangibility of the sukuk drops below this, then certain remedial steps must be taken. If tangibility drops below 33 per cent, then steps must be taken to prevent any secondary market trading of the sukuk (including delisting the sukuk in the event it is listed on a stock exchange).

- Intangible receivables can no longer be used as the basis for structuring sukuk. An Islamic bank will have made retail and corporate Islamic loans to customers/clients using the *murabaha* mode of financing. Historically, an Islamic bank that may have wanted to issue a sukuk would have used these *murabaha* financial assets, which are receivables only, as part of the assets for any sukuk it may issue. This is no longer permitted. Additionally, other intangible assets such as assets during construction (referred to as *istisna*) are also not permitted.

- Whilst the use of a *murabaha* component in a *wakala* sukuk is still permitted[2] (provided the overall tangibility ratio is not breached), the *murabaha* portion of the sukuk cannot be

---

2   The Issuer SPV will use part of the issuance proceeds to buy commodities and then on-sell them to the Obligor for a deferred payment price. This is different from where the Obligor has *murabaha* receivables on its balance sheet and sells these to the Issuer SPV. For further details, please see *sukuk-al-wakala* set out in Chapter 4 at Part 4.4.

structured on the basis of a floating profit rate. The profit rate on the *murabaha* must be fixed, which introduces further complexities for floating rate sukuk. As a result, floating rate mechanics have essentially been removed from the vast majority of sukuk transactions.

In addition to AAOIFI Standard No. 59, the applicability of AAOIFI Sharia Standards generally has resulted in a number of refinements to established structures and documents, including, as follows:

- Enhanced service agency mechanics;
- Rent reduction for partial loss on *ijara* deals;
- Sharia rationale for indemnity payment instead of the payment of exercise price; and
- Requirement to appoint a sharia advisor for the issuance.

Further details on these and other developments are set out in Chapter 6 (*Recent Developments*). In addition, for a more general overview of some of the key principles applicable to Islamic finance, see Appendix (*Overview of Key Principles of Islamic Finance*).

CHAPTER 2

ROLE OF PARTIES

BEFORE WE DISCUSS the underlying Islamic and commercial structures, it is worth discussing and clarifying the roles of the parties involved in a sukuk transaction and the terminology that is used.

2.1. Sharia Scholar

A sukuk transaction must be approved as sharia-compliant by a sharia scholar or a group of sharia scholars. The sharia scholar(s) will issue a fatwa (or pronouncement) which will confirm that, from their perspective, the sukuk structure and the sukuk documents are sharia-compliant.

The identity of the sharia scholar(s) that will issue this pronouncement is dependent on the parties involved.

If the Obligor (i.e. the entity to which there is credit recourse) is a sharia-compliant entity such as an Islamic bank/financial institution, this confirmation will be provided by the sharia board of the Obligor. The banks which are acting as joint lead managers will also, to the extent they have a sharia board, also issue a pronouncement. When the Obligor elects to raise financing on a sharia-compliant basis (but is not obliged to do so) but none of the joint lead managers has a sharia board, then the Obligor may appoint an independent sharia consultant to provide this service.

It is critical that a pronouncement is issued prior to the launch of the sukuk as potential Islamic investors will want to know that the proposed transaction has been approved as sharia compliant and will also want to know by which scholar. The pronouncement will be used to provide comfort to potential Islamic investors during the marketing of the sukuk as to its sharia compliance (albeit the pronouncement is issued for 'comfort' and on a non-reliance basis for potential investors). In the event the Obligor is a sharia-compliant entity, then this pronouncement is required for its own internal governance purposes as well.

In recent years – and with the growing sophistication of the market – regulators in certain jurisdictions will also require the sharia compliance of a sukuk to be confirmed by the issue of a pronouncement before it can be marketed to investors in its jurisdiction. This is the case in the UAE (as required by the HSA) and also the case in Malaysia (a requirement of the Securities Commission).

Whilst the pronouncement that is issued is made available to investors, it is disclosed on the basis that it is a subjective interpretation of the sharia board that has issued the fatwa, and that an investor cannot rely on it and must make their own subjective determination of sharia compliance. The pronouncement that is issued will however lead investors to look at which individual scholars have issued the fatwa, and this will, in turn, facilitate their own internal sharia approvals, where required.

Whilst, historically, the sharia board only used to have a role prior to the issuance of the sukuk, which was limited to reviewing the sukuk structure and the transaction documents, its role and involvement whilst an issuance remains outstanding is growing.

Where the Obligor has its own sharia board, it will be involved in reviewing the ongoing sukuk as part of the usual annual sharia audit. However, where the Obligor does not have its own sharia board, there is a requirement for a sharia board to be appointed during the life of the transaction in certain circumstances. This could include where (i) the sukuk assets may change so the sharia board is responsible for checking the sharia compliance of the trust assets; and (ii) the tangibility of the trust assets drops below a certain pre-agreed level, which will require certain remedial action to be taken. This level could be 51 or 33 per cent depending on the jurisdiction and the nature of the remedial action required. Under AAOIFI Standard No. 59, if a sukuk drops below 51 per cent, the Obligor should consult with the sharia board to take the necessary steps to bring the tangibility back to 51 per cent.

2.2. Obligor

The Obligor on a sukuk transaction is the commercial entity to which there is primary recourse or, in the example of a securitisation sukuk, is the entity that sells/transfers the securitisation assets to the Issuer. The Obligor is sometimes referred to as an Originator in a securitisation sukuk and is referred to as the Issuer in a conventional bond transaction. The terms Obligor and Issuer are used interchangeably by market participants but for the purposes of this book, I have kept them separate.

2.3. Issuer

The Issuer will act as the trustee for the investors and therefore it is essentially a conduit vehicle on behalf of the investors. The Issuer will take instructions from the investors when required, in accordance with the terms and conditions of the sukuk. The Issuer on a sukuk transaction will usually be a special purpose vehicle (referred to as an SPV) that has been established in a jurisdiction that recognises the concept of a trust. The Issuer will delegate its rights to a professional trustee company, which is referred to as a Delegate. The Delegate is contractually empowered to exercise rights on behalf of the Issuer.

As a consequence, sukuk transactions will often involve an Issuer located in offshore jurisdictions such as the Cayman Islands, Jersey, Malaysia (including Labuan), and in recent years, the Dubai International Financial Centre (DIFC) and the Abu Dhabi Global Markets (ADGM). This is not an exhaustive list and other jurisdictions may also be used, subject to the legal, tax and regulatory analysis of a particular transaction. In my own experience, I have used SPVs that have been set up in offshore jurisdictions such as the Cayman Islands, Bermuda, Jersey, DIFC and ADGM, as well as onshore common law jurisdictions where the concept of a trust is recognised, such as the United Kingdom, and also onshore civil law jurisdictions where specific legislation may have been enacted to recognise a trust (or equivalent interest) in the context of a sukuk issuance, for example, Indonesia and Turkey.

The principal reason why the Issuer is an SPV is to segregate the obligations of the Obligor from the obligations of the Issuer from an Islamic perspective. As we will see further in Chapter 4 (*Sukuk Structures*), the Obligor will enter into an Islamic finance instrument with the Issuer to provide a sharia basis for the payments that will be used to fund coupon and principal payments to investors. An Obligor, for example, cannot enter into an *ijara* or a *mudaraba* with itself, and therefore an SPV is required as the counterparty.

There is one notable exception to the use of either an offshore or onshore SPV, which is domestic sukuk transactions in the Kingdom of Saudi Arabia. Domestic sukuk transactions in Saudi Arabia do not use a separate SPV nor do they use the common law concept of trust. This is specific to the domestic market in Saudi Arabia, where the corporate entity that is proposing to issue sukuk (i.e. Company 'X') can, in certain circumstances, act in multiple different legal capacities such as Obligor and Issuer, and this is recognised under the laws of Saudi Arabia as being enforceable.

One question that is often raised is in respect of the ownership of the SPV? The general rule is that the SPV should be an orphan vehicle: in other words, the shares of the SPV are held in charitable trust, which maintains the integrity of independence between the Obligor and the Issuer. However, there are exceptional reasons in some transactions where the SPV, although a separate legal entity, may be owned by the Obligor itself. This is usually used on sovereign transactions where, because of public policy reasons, the government cannot transfer or convey public assets to a non-governmental entity. Outside of the sovereign space – whilst there may sometimes be commercial reasons to set up the SPV as a subsidiary of the Obligor rather than as an orphan vehicle – this approach is not usually endorsed by the sharia scholars.

2.4. Delegate

As mentioned above, since the Issuer is an SPV, it will appoint and delegate its rights to a professional trustee company, referred to as a Delegate, which is contractually empowered to exercise rights on behalf of the Issuer SPV. The Delegate will take instructions from the investors where required, in accordance with the terms and conditions of the sukuk, and will often be privy to the transaction documents to allow it to exercise rights on behalf of the Issuer, where needed. The Delegate is appointed under a document referred to as the declaration of trust.

2.5. Listing Agent

Sukuk can be both listed and unlisted. The rationale for an Obligor to decide whether to list a sukuk is the same as the rationale that is adopted for determining whether a bond should be listed.

The usual position is that a listed sukuk will be of interest to a wider potential investor base, including investors such as pension funds or insurance companies that may in certain jurisdictions only be permitted to invest in listed instruments. A listed sukuk will however need to adhere to a minimum standard of disclosure and often ongoing reporting requirements – the disclosure is not just the summary of the Islamic structure but also key information in respect of the Obligor, including what it does, what the key risks are to its business or jurisdictions of operation, its internal decision-making processes, corporate governance, and so on. In essence, all the key information that a prudent investor would want to know before making an investment decision on whether to invest in any potential sukuk offering by an Obligor.

When a decision is made to list a sukuk, this will then involve various third parties, including the relevant exchange where the sukuk is to be listed and, depending on the exchange involved, also a Listing Agent. A common misconception is that a listed sukuk is traded on-exchange, but this is not correct. A stock exchange for a listed sukuk (in the same way as a listed conventional bond) simply provides comfort that the disclosure meets certain standards as required by the exchange's regulatory framework. Any secondary market trading of that sukuk will still involve an 'over-the-counter' transaction between a buyer, a seller and often a broker who facilitates that transaction.

2.6. Rating Agency

A Rating Agency can assist with providing more transparency on the credit risk of a sukuk. Comparable to conventional bond issuance, a recognised rating of the Obligor can improve the marketability of the relevant sukuk. It is possible for either the Obligor to be rated or for the sukuk issuance itself to be rated, or both. All of the three large international rating agencies – S&P, Moody's and Fitch – provide rating services for sukuk issuances. An advantage of the involvement of a credit rating agency is that certain institutional investors can only invest in rated instruments. Therefore, the credit rating will indicate the scale of the credit risk that an investor is taking by investing in that sukuk. However, the credit rating is not an indication of the level of sharia compliance.

2.7. Registrar

A Registrar is appointed by the Issuer and assists with maintaining a register of investors that shows: (i) the outstanding face amount of certificates represented by the global certificate (and being empowered to register the global certificate in the name of the common depositary); (ii) any definitive certificates have been issued, any serial numbers and the date of issue of any such certificates; (iii) all subsequent transfers and change of ownership of any certificates; (iv) the payment of all periodic distribution amounts and amounts in the nature of principal under the certificates; (v) address and bank details of the investors and the principal amount of sukuk held by each investor; and (vi) any increases or decreases in the aggregate principal amount outstanding of sukuk, following early redemption or buyback.

The Registrar is empowered to exchange the global certificate (held in the name of the common depositary) for definitive certificates (in the name of each investor). This will only be required if there is a market disruption event that impacts the global certificate.

2.8. Calculation Agent

In the event a calculation of a periodic distribution amount is required (such as on floating rate instruments), then this will be performed by the Calculation Agent. A Calculation Agent is not required for a fixed rate transaction.

2.9. Transfer Agent

The Issuer will also appoint a Transfer Agent, which will assist with the transfer of any definitive certificate that may have been issued by the Registrar.

2.10. Principal Paying Agent

The Paying Agent is an agent of the Issuer and provides administrative support, including obtaining the International Securities Identification Number (ISIN) for each programme drawdown (this is the one-off responsibility of the lead arranger in a standalone sukuk), and collecting funds from the Obligor on the payment date and remitting them as coupon and redemption payments to investors. For global note sukuk, this payment is made by the Paying Agent to the common depositary/ICSD, which then credits each investors' currency account held with it. In the case of definitive sukuk, the payment is made upon presentation by the investor of the coupon. Upon the occurrence of certain events that are referred to as dissolution events, or potential dissolution events, the Delegate usually has the power to direct the Principal Paying Agent to act as an agent of the Delegate, rather than the Trustee and this authority is given to the Delegate in the paying agency agreement.

2.11. Lead Manager

The Lead Manager is the entity (usually a financial institution) that is involved in arranging, structuring and distributing the issuance on behalf of the Obligor.

CHAPTER 3

COMMERCIAL VARIATIONS OF SUKUK

BEFORE DISCUSSING THE different Islamic structures that are available to facilitate the structuring of a sukuk, it is first worth touching upon the different varieties of sukuk that are available commercially. I do not mean which underlying Islamic structure will be used (this will be explored in more detail in the next chapter), but rather the intended commercial structure and the legal rights and recourse that the proposed investors will have. These can broadly be split into the following categories:

- Senior unsecured sukuk
- Senior secured sukuk
- Covered sukuk
- Securitisation sukuk
- Regulatory capital sukuk
- Hybrid/perpetual sukuk
- Convertible and exchangeable sukuk

This list is not definitive, and it is possible to structure sukuk which may have some commercial features that straddle across more than one of these categories, but this distinction is nevertheless helpful. I will take a look at each of these in more detail to provide an overview of the key commercial feature.

3.1. Senior Unsecured Sukuk

This is the most common type of sukuk that is issued in the market. A senior unsecured sukuk is an instrument whereby the investors – assuming the instrument is structured correctly from a legal and regulatory perspective – are taking only the credit risk of the Obligor. Whether an investor receives its payment of profit (i.e. a coupon payment) or repayment of principal, is entirely dependent upon the overall performance of the Obligor's business. The Obligor can use any portion of its overall income to make its payment obligations to investors. If the Obligor's business fails or is impacted in a way that disrupts its cash flow or income, an investor will not have any recourse to the physical assets of the Obligor but will need to stand in line with every other senior unsecured creditor. In the worst-case scenario where the Obligor is insolvent, all senior unsecured creditors – irrespective of what type of debt instrument they have invested in – will all be treated equally. The insolvency rules vary depending on the jurisdiction, but generally, this will include all senior unsecured bondholders, all senior unsecured sukuk investors, all unsecured Islamic and conventional loan creditors, as well as all trade creditors.

These are often referred to as asset-based sukuk because the sukuk has an Islamic structure that underpins the instrument so that the cash flow from the Obligor is based on one of the structures set out in Chapter 4 (*Sukuk Structures*), but the Islamic structure is to justify the cash flow and payments from an Islamic perspective. In a senior unsecured sukuk, therefore, given it is asset-based only, the investors can never seize or enforce against the sukuk assets themselves. This is a very important nuance that is often overlooked and misunderstood.

3.2. Senior Secured Sukuk

With this instrument, the obligation of the Obligor to pay a particular amount is secured by way of security/collateral granted by the Obligor, which would need to be perfect in the normal course in accordance with domestic security/collateral laws. The security/collateral could be granted over the assets that are used to structure the sukuk (see further for the covered sukuk) or could be over assets that are not used to underpin the Islamic structure. A good example would be, if an Obligor has issued a sukuk using certain real estate that it owns (e.g. real estate asset 'A'), the Obligor may grant a mortgage over completely separate real estate that it owns (e.g. real estate asset 'B') as security for its payment obligations. If the Obligor fails to make the necessary payments in due time, investors could then commence proceedings to enforce their rights including enforcing against real estate asset 'B'. The investors would, assuming the security/collateral has been granted properly, have first and priority recourse to real estate asset 'B' in the event the Obligor was to go insolvent.

So why would an Obligor issue a senior secured sukuk rather than a senior unsecured instrument? This is purely a commercially driven matter based on the creditworthiness of the Obligor. If the Obligor is viewed as being a high credit risk (i.e. a higher chance of it defaulting on its payment obligations), then investors may well expect to be granted security until all payment obligations have been discharged and the sukuk has been redeemed.

3.3. Covered Sukuk

A covered sukuk is a sub-set of a senior secured sukuk and is an instrument whereby the obligation of the Obligor to pay is secured by the assets that are used to underpin the Islamic structure. A good example would be, if an Obligor has issued a *sukuk-al-ijara* (see Chapter 4 *Sukuk Structures* for more details) using certain real estate that it owns (e.g. real estate asset 'A'), security may be granted over that real estate 'A' in favour of the investors. If the Obligor fails to make the necessary payments by the time they are due, investors could then commence proceedings to enforce against real estate asset 'A'. The investors would have first ranking priority recourse to real estate asset 'A' in the event the Obligor was to go insolvent. In the event any proceeds of enforcement of real estate asset 'A' were insufficient to discharge the full amount of the debt outstanding to the investors, it would still have an unsecured claim for the difference against the Obligor.

3.4. Securitisation Sukuk

Here is where the commercial structure really gets interesting! A securitisation sukuk is an asset-backed structure – the Obligor will convey (either by way of sale or transfer or another equivalent concept) to the investors certain revenue-generating assets. These assets, and the cash flow generated by these assets, will belong to the investors. Securitisation sukuks are usually – although there are commercial exceptions to this – set up such that investors do not have recourse to the other assets or cash flow of the Obligor (in other words, the Obligor is not obliged to use its other income/revenue to pay the investors that have invested in the securitisation sukuk). If the sukuk assets do not generate the intended cash flow, there is usually no recourse to the Obligor at all.

The analysis that is done for a securitisation sukuk is very different from a sukuk where there is credit recourse to the Obligor. For a securitisation sukuk, the focus and analysis are on the proposed sukuk assets and the cash flow they generate, as well as the robustness of the conveyance of the proposed sukuk assets by the Obligor to the Issuer to ensure that this conveyance cannot be challenged by a liquidator upon subsequent insolvency of the Obligor. As the focus is on the assets being transferred and the revenue stream, the financial modelling completed prior to a securitisation sukuk is critical to ensure sufficient cash will be generated by the sukuk assets to pay profit/coupon and repayment of principal to investors (and often with some 'headroom' or cushion).

So, what are the reasons and advantages for an Obligor to issue a securitisation sukuk? And given this sounds like the optimum instrument from an Islamic perspective, why are there so few of these issued?

Whilst the auditing and accounting rules will vary from jurisdiction to jurisdiction, generally, a securitisation sukuk will be 'off balance sheet'. This means that the Obligor can take the assets which are being securitised off its balance sheet completely. It also often means that an Obligor may have a cost of funding which would be cheaper than a senior unsecured instrument, particularly where the Obligor may have a low credit rating.

There are, however, several reasons why an Obligor may not want to do a securitisation: ranging from the emotive reason of a reduction in balance sheet size to the inadequacy of the insolvency laws. A securitisation will require investors to be comfortable that in the event the Obligor was to go insolvent, the liquidator of the Obligor would not be able to take the securitised assets back. A mature sophisticated legal environment is required with a comprehensive insolvency law, which for many jurisdictions where Obligors may want to issue securitisation sukuk is often lacking or not sufficiently robust or tested. Additionally, Islamic investors that would want to buy a securitisation sukuk are very limited – most traditional Islamic investors require recourse back to the Obligor. Securitisation issuances are usually purchased by sophisticated investors that recognise and appreciate the difference between a senior secured/unsecured sukuk and a securitisation instrument.

By way of anecdote, when I was working on my first USD global sukuk in 2003, the original intention was to undertake a securitisation sukuk. However, during the pre-marketing phase, all the investors made it clear that they wanted to have the Obligor 'back-stop' the deal. In other words, if the assets that were proposed to be securitised did not perform, they wanted to have recourse back to the Obligor. So, the securitisation sukuk was then replaced with a senior unsecured sukuk which formed the basis of the first global sukuk issuance by the Islamic Development Bank.

3.5. Regulatory Capital Sukuk

A regulatory capital sukuk is specific to the world of Islamic banks and financial institutions. It is also asset-based, so the Islamic structure is used to ensure the cash flow is sharia-compliant, and there is recourse back to the Obligor. However, the Obligor's obligation to pay and the investors' recourse is subordinated to the payment of that Obligor's senior liabilities. So, essentially an investor purchasing a regulatory capital sukuk is treated as having greater rights than a shareholder of the Obligor, but fewer rights than an investor that holds a senior secured/unsecured instrument issued by that Obligor. A regulatory capital sukuk is closer to a risk-sharing instrument. For those of you who are more familiar with the world of regulatory capital, there are degrees of regulatory capital, and this is no different in the Islamic finance world. There is what is known as 'Tier 1 capital' and 'Tier 2 capital'. Without getting into the technicalities of regulatory capital and the prudential standards that govern the regulatory capital of banks, a Tier 1 issuance is closer in risk and reward to equity than a Tier 2 issuance.

3.6. Hybrid/Perpetual Sukuk

A hybrid or perpetual sukuk is issued by Obligors that are non-bank/financial institutions, and the primary reason to issue such a sukuk is that it is usually treated from an Obligor's accounting perspective as equity or equity-like, rather than a liability/debt. The determination of whether the sukuk will have equity classification or a liability classification is an accounting question, which will vary as per the accounting standards adopted in a specific jurisdiction. However, a perpetual sukuk will either not have a maturity date or will include a mechanism whereby there is an increase in the profit rate payable to investors if the sukuk is not redeemed by the Obligor after the specified period from the issuance date, e.g. every 10 years.

A hybrid/perpetual sukuk is also asset-based, so the Islamic structure is used for the purposes of ensuring the cash flow is sharia-compliant, and there is recourse back to the Obligor.

The Obligor usually cannot pay the coupon on a perpetual sukuk unless all its senior liabilities are current. Even if senior liabilities are current (i.e. all senior liabilities have been paid up to the proposed payment under the perpetual sukuk), the Obligor may elect not to pay the coupon to the investors. A decision not to pay the coupon will have certain consequences depending on whether it is a 'cumulative' perpetual sukuk or a 'non-cumulative' perpetual sukuk. Consequences can include capitalising the unpaid coupon, non-payment of the coupon triggering a dividend blocker for the Obligor (i.e. the Obligor may not declare a dividend in favour of its shareholders if it elects to not pay a coupon), and so on.

A hybrid/perpetual sukuk is usually a subordinated sukuk, which means that it is essentially equity-like (similar to a regulatory capital sukuk) and investors will rank behind senior secured/unsecured investors. It is possible to structure a perpetual sukuk as a senior perpetual where the coupon payment may be a senior liability and the payment of principal is subordinated, or the payment obligation is subordinated unless the Obligor goes insolvent, in which case the obligation becomes a senior obligation. There is a large degree of commercial flexibility depending on the applicable accounting standards.

A perpetual sukuk is usually an expensive form of capital for an Obligor, so these are quite rarely issued. However, they do nevertheless exist and play an important role where an Obligor needs to increase the equity side of its balance sheet but is unable to raise further shareholders' equity.

3.7. Convertible and Exchangeable Sukuk

These terms are often used interchangeably but there is a difference. They are commercially structured as senior unsecured sukuk that can be converted into equity of either the Obligor (convertible) or the equity of third party (exchangeable) upon the occurrence of certain pre-agreed trigger events and in a pre-agreed conversion ratio. However, these are also asset-based sukuk, and investors have no recourse to the assets that are used to underpin the Islamic structure. The assets are used solely for the purposes of justifying the cash flow payable to the investor from an Islamic perspective.

As you will have noted above, aside from securitisation sukuk where investors generally have no recourse to the Obligor, all other sukuk will involve the investor having recourse to the Obligor either in full or, in the case of a senior secured or covered sukuk, for any shortfall that may remain following enforcement. Therefore, most auditors will treat sukuk as a financial liability and a debt of the Obligor on its financial statements.

The table here will help summarise the commentary above:

COMMERCIAL TYPE OF SUKUK	ASSET BASED OR ASSET BACKED	RECOURSE TO THE OBLIGOR	RECOURSE TO THE ASSETS UNDERPINNING THE SUKUK
Senior Unsecured Sukuk	Asset-based	Yes	No
Senior Secured Sukuk	Asset-based	Yes	Only to the extent the sukuk assets are also the secured assets, otherwise recourse to the secured assets
Covered Sukuk	Asset-based	Yes	Yes, although through the enforcement of security
Securitisation Sukuk	Asset-backed	No[3]	Yes
Regulatory Capital Sukuk	Asset-based	Yes	No
Hybrid/Perpetual Sukuk	Asset-based	Yes	No
Convertible Sukuk	Asset-based	Yes	No
Exchangeable Sukuk	Asset-based	Yes	No

---

3   Whilst the general rule is that there is no recourse to the Obligor, certain securitisation transactions may be commercially structured such that the first loss of underlying cash flow (up to a certain percentage) is absorbed by the Obligor, so in these situations there is limited recourse to the Obligor.

For those sukuk that provide recourse to the Obligor, the 'honeycomb' diagram below is a useful example of ranking. The higher the ranking of an investor on an Obligor's insolvency, the lower the cost of capital for the Obligor. Equally, the lower the ranking of an investor on an Obligor's insolvency, the higher the cost of capital for the Obligor.

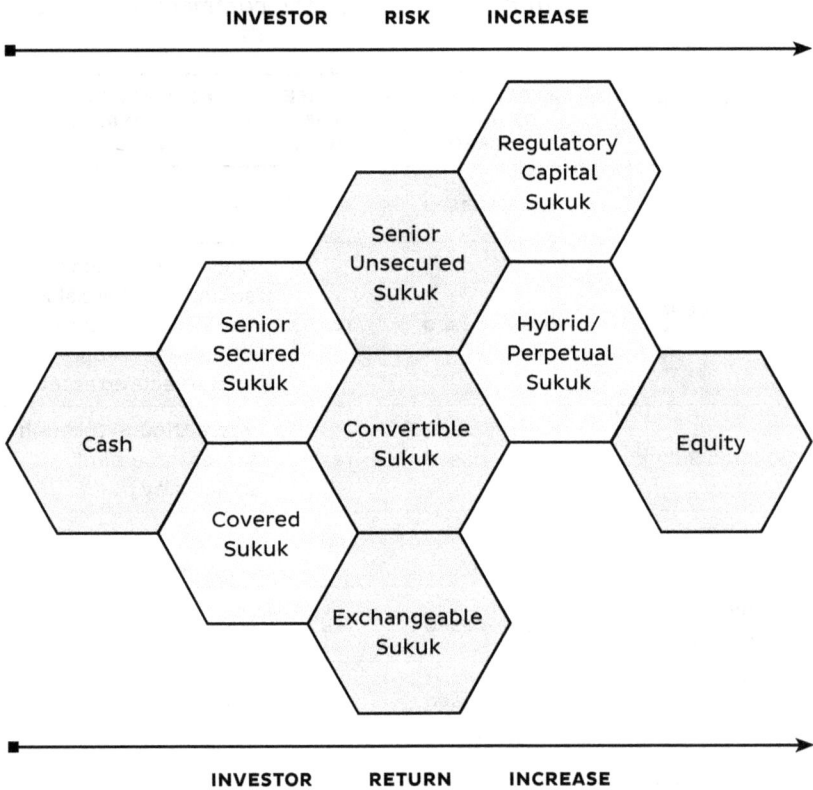

Figure 3.1: A honeycomb diagram showing an example of investor ranking.

CHAPTER 4

SUKUK

STRUCTURES

WE WILL NOW TAKE a closer look at the Islamic structures that are used in sukuk transactions in the context of cross border international sukuk transactions. I have sought to focus on international transactions as when structuring a cross border transaction the key is to ensure that the structure will be acceptable to the widest investor base possible to ensure the success of the transaction. Domestic transactions may follow a slightly different route and structure dependent upon the sharia requirements and legal environment of a specific jurisdiction, so the structures set out in this chapter are based on the premise that the structure is to accommodate an international or cross border deal.

This is often the most debated part of any transaction and whilst the commercial aspects are agreed between the Obligor, its financial advisers and the lead managers, the next phase of the discussion is ensuring the commercial aspects of the structure can be implemented in a sharia compliant manner and this will involve discussions with the sharia scholars.

The Islamic structure will involve the use of an underlying Islamic finance instrument which I will look at in more detail, and I will then take a look at how the market has evolved in the last few years to accommodate for what has become known as hybrid structures.

SUKUK STRUCTURE	PERCENTAGE OF REQUIRED ASSETS	ACCEPTABILITY	ADVANTAGES	DISADVANTAGES
Mudaraba Part 4.1	No pre-identified assets for general business *mudaraba*	Global	No transfer of asset required	Cannot be used for secured or senior unsecured or covered sukuk
Ijara Part 4.2	Assets equivalent to 100% of issuance amount	Global	Globally accepted and approved	Assets equivalent to issuance amount required
Murabaha Part 4.3	0% assets required from Obligor	Cannot involve a UAE based Lead Manager	Obligor not required to use any of its own assets	Limited acceptability
Wakala Part 4.4	51% tangibility	Global	Only 51% tangibility required Profit generated from tangible and non-tangible assets	More time consuming to document

One final point to note before we get into the detail is that sukuk can be issued in standalone format (i.e. a single transaction), or an Obligor can put in place a sukuk programme i.e. a platform which allows the Obligor to issue sukuk as and when required. The documentary requirements for a programme are slightly different than a standalone sukuk issuance, so for ease of simplicity the focus below will primarily be on standalone issuances and the Islamic structuring issues that arise when structuring standalone sukuk issuances.

Before going through the details of each structure, I thought it would be helpful to set out a tabular form some key features of each structure.

The table on the previous page helps to summarise the key features of each structure and the advantages and disadvantages.

4.1. Sukuk-al-mudaraba

The term *mudaraba* is broadly understood to refer to a form of partnership arrangement whereby one partner provides capital (and such partner is referred to as the *rab-al-maal*) and the other partner provides managerial and investment skills (and this partner is referred to as the *Mudarib*). The *Mudarib* applies its expertise to invest the capital to generate a return for both the partners. The *mudaraba* can be either:

- The overall business of the Obligor (provided the Obligor is a sharia compliant entity), so for example an Islamic financial institution could act as a *Mudarib* using its entire business;
- A specific part of the business of the Obligor (again provided that such specific part is sharia compliant business); or
- A completely independent and separate enterprise from the Obligor's own business.

45

At this point I would note that *sukuk-al-mudaraba* do have a contentious history. Whilst at its core a *mudaraba* is intended to provide 'equity type risk' so is ideal for the structuring of regulatory capital sukuk and hybrid/perpetual sukuk, this structure was prior to 2008 also being used to structure senior unsecured sukuk transactions. This was being achieved by the Obligor granting to the Issuer SPV a purchase undertaking to oblige the Obligor to purchase from the Issuer SPV its ownership interest in the *Mudaraba* Assets at a pre-agreed exercise price formulation. This practice was

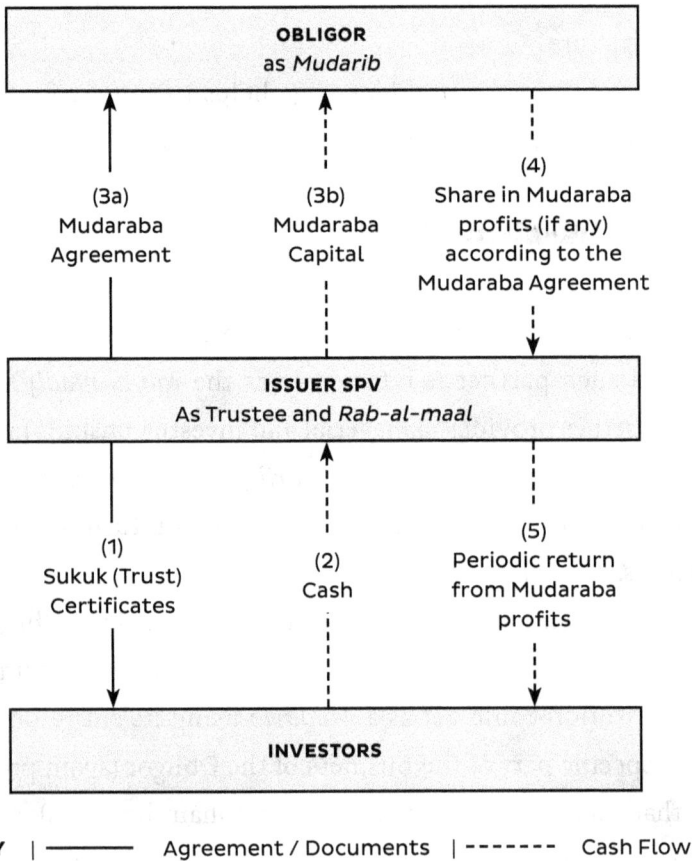

Figure 4.1: Structure of Sukuk-al-mudaraba

disapproved of by AAOIFI in 2008 and has not been used in the market since then (although some pre-2008 legacy deals may remain).

Whilst at the time this did not impact sukuk that were already issued, it did prevent future senior unsecured transactions from using this structure. It also led to the Dana Gas litigation in 2016 where the Obligor sought to argue that the sukuk was non-sharia compliant and therefore it had no obligation to repay the principal in full.

Sukuk-al-mudaraba are still used for the structuring of equity risk instrument (i.e. hybrid instruments) and regulatory capital sukuk issued by financial institutions. Figure 4.1 is an example of a typical *sukuk-al-mudaraba* structure.

4.1.1. Overview of Sukuk–al–mudaraba Structure

(Using the numbering from Figure 4.1 on page 46)

(1) The Issuer SPV issues *sukuk,* which for international transactions will be way of declaration of trust. The Issuer SPV, once the trust has been declared, will be acting as Issuer and Trustee and will hold all its assets and rights from time to time on trust for the investors. The sukuk provides an investor with a right against the Issuer to certain payments, namely the economic return on the sukuk (which is often referred to as the coupon or the periodic distribution amount) and the return of capital (which is often referred to as the redemption amount or dissolution amount).

(2) The investors subscribe for sukuk and pay the proceeds to Issuer SPV (the Issuance Proceeds). The Issuer SPV declares a trust over the Issuance Proceeds (and any investment made using the Issuance Proceeds) and thereby acts as Trustee on behalf of the investors.

(3a) The Obligor, as *Mudarib* under the *Mudaraba* Agreement, agrees to contribute its expertise and management skills to the sharia compliant *Mudaraba*, with responsibility for managing the *rab-al-maal*'s cash contribution (i.e. *Mudaraba* Capital) in accordance with specified investment parameters as set out in the *Mudaraba* Agreement or an investment plan agreed between the *Mudarib* and the *rab-al-maal*.

(3b) Issuer SPV and the Obligor enter into a *Mudaraba* Agreement with the Obligor as *Mudarib* and Issuer SPV as *rab-al-maal*. In accordance with the *Mudaraba* Agreement, the Issuer SPV agrees to contribute the Issuance Proceeds for the purpose of a sharia compliant *Mudaraba*, or in other words the *Mudareb* will manage and invest the Principal Amount contributed by the *rab-al-maal*. This contribution is referred to as the '*Mudaraba* Capital'.

(4) The profits generated by the *Mudaraba* are divided between Issuer SPV (as *rab-al-maal*) and Obligor (as *Mudarib*) in accordance with the profit-sharing ratios set out in the *Mudaraba* Agreement. It is important that the *Mudarib* is not paid a fixed fee as a *mudaraba* needs to be distinguished from an agency relationship (where a fixed fee is possible) as the *Mudarib* should only financially benefit from the profits generated by the *Mudaraba*.

A fixed income investor would want to ensure that it receives a fixed coupon under the Sukuk certificates. How is this then achieved by an underlying Islamic structure which may itself be generating a variable return?

The *Mudaraba* profit-sharing ratio is agreed such that the majority of the *Mudaraba* profits are for the benefit of the *rab-al-maal*, so for example the *Mudaraba* Agreement may stipulate that the profit-sharing ratio between the *rab-al-maal* and the *Mudarib* should be 90:10 i.e. for every USD 100 of profit generated by the *Mudaraba*, the *rab-al-maal* is entitled to USD 90 and the *Mudarib* is entitled to USD 10. However if the 90 per cent profit share results in a *rab-al-maal* receiving an amount (in aggregate) which is greater than what the Issuer SPV is obliged to pay under the Sukuk Certificates (in aggregate), the *rab-al-maal* will forego the difference in favour of the *Mudarib* as an incentive fee on maturity of the Sukuk (and the liquidation of the *Mudaraba*).

If the *Mudarib* does not generate enough profit (so the 90 per cent of the Profit which the *Mudarib* is entitled to is lower than the coupon amount the Issuer SPV is obliged to pay to investors) then that is the risk that the investors take. The investors are not entitled to anymore than the pre-agreed 90 per cent profit share, hence why investors are taking 'equity like' risk.

If we look at a practical example: The Obligor wishes to raise USD 10 million to fund a specific project and the expected rate of return of the project for investors is 10 per cent. The Obligor decides to utilise a *mudaraba* arrangement to raise the capital. The Issuer SPV issues USD 10 million of Sukuk Certificates which will therefore pay a return of 10 per cent to investors (i.e. USD 1 million).

If the project generates a return of 15 per cent (i.e. USD 1.5 million), under the *Mudaraba* Agreement the *rab-al-maal* is entitled to 90 per cent of this profit i.e. USD 1.35 million. However the *rab-al-maal* will have pre-agreed that any amount raised in excess of the USD 1 million will be given to the *Mudarib* as an incentive fee. So the *rab-al-maal* (and therefore the investors) will receive USD 1 million as return and the *Mudarib* will receive USD 0.5 million as a combination of its share of the *Mudaraba* Profit (i.e. 10 per cent of USD 1.5 million i.e. USD 150,000 and the incentive fee i.e. USD 350,000, so a total of USD 0.5 million.

If the project generates a return of 5 per cent (i.e. USD 0.5 million), under the *Mudaraba* Agreement the *rab-al-maal* is entitled to 90 per cent of this profit i.e. USD 0.45 million. and the *Mudarib* is entitled to 10 per cent of the profit i.e. USD 0.05 million. The investors are not entitled to more than their share of the *Mudaraba* profit. This is therefore the risk which the investors are taking – hence why the investors are taking 'equity like' risk. The investors are not equity investors (i.e. they are not shareholders) but their return is premised on the success of the *Mudaraba* project, in the same way the dividend payment to shareholders is premised on the Obligor making a profit and generating a return.

The profit/loss calculations can be carried out on the maturity/dissolution of the *Mudaraba*, so any periodic payments of surplus *mudaraba* profit and any periodic *mudaraba* losses can be looked at as a whole to avoid the *Mudarib* unfairly benefitting from extra profits during one periodic distribution period.

Issuer SPV receives the *Mudaraba* profits and holds them as Trustee on behalf of the investors. Issuer SPV (as Trustee) pays each periodic return to investors using the *Mudaraba* profits it has received under the *Mudaraba* Agreement.

Although the profits generated during the term of the *Mudaraba* are accrued for distribution on dissolution at maturity, period distributions to investors may nonetheless be achieved during the term of the *sukuk* issuance through payments of 'advance profits'. This would typically be effected by way of a constructive liquidation of the *Mudaraba* assets at specified intervals whereby the amounts of advance profit would represent the difference between:

i   the market value of the *Mudaraba* assets on the relevant constructive liquidation date; and

ii the original value of the *Mudaraba* assets on the issuance date.

4.1.2. Key Features of the Mudaraba Structure

Set out below is a summary of the basic requirements which should be considered when using mudaraba as the underlying structure for the issuance of *sukuk*:

- Obligor (as *Mudarib*) discharges and performs its obligations under the *Mudaraba* Agreement with the degree of skill and care that it would exercise in respect of its own assets.

- An investment plan in respect of the *Mudaraba* enterprise will be tailored within sharia parameters to meet the financing objectives of the *sukuk-al-mudaraba* as set out in the *Mudaraba* Agreement.

- The *Mudaraba* may be entered into on a restricted basis whereby the Obligor (as *Mudarib*) must invest the sukuk proceeds in accordance with the specified investment plan or maybe entered into on an unrestricted basis.

- The profit-sharing ratio between Issuer SPV (as *rab-al-maal*) and Obligor (as *Mudarib*) must be agreed at the time of the conclusion of *Mudaraba* Agreement. This cannot be expressed as a rate based on each party's contribution in the *Mudaraba* enterprise nor as a pre-agreed lump sum but a portion of mudaraba profit only.

- Any capital losses of the *Mudaraba* would be borne by Issuer SPV (as *rab-al-maal*), although its liabilities are limited to proceeds invested (therefore, investors would not be liable for more than their investment into the *sukuk-al-mudaraba*).

4.1.3. Required Islamic Documentation for Sukuk–al-mudaraba

The Islamic documentation on the next page is typically required for a *sukuk-al-mudaraba* transaction:

DOCUMENT	PARTIES	SUMMARY / PURPOSE
Mudaraba Agreement	Obligor (as *Mudarib*) and Issuer SPV (as *rab-al-maal*)	Sets out the terms of the *Mudaraba* under which the Issuer SPV shall invest the Principal Amount and prescribes the profit-sharing ratios between the parties

4.1.4. Required Capital Market Documentation for Sukuk-al-mudaraba

The following underlying capital market documentation is typically required for a *sukuk-al-mudaraba* transaction:

DOCUMENT	PARTIES	SUMMARY / PURPOSE
Prospectus (including terms & conditions)		The Prospectus will set out key risk factors, disclosure on the Obligor and Issuer SPV as well as key other information that investors need to be aware of as part of making an informed investment decision
Declaration of Trust	Issuer SPV, Obligor and Delegate	Creation of the trust certificates and appointment of Delegate and empowering delegate to take certain actions under certain circumstances e.g. Obligor default
Agency Agreement	Issuer SPV, Obligor, Delegate, Paying Agent, Transfer Agent, Calculation Agent	Appointment of Agents
Subscription Agreement	Issuer SPV, Obligor, Joint Lead Managers	Subscription of the Sukuk by the Joint Lead Managers

4.2. Sukuk-al-ijara

The most commonly used *sukuk* structure globally is that of *sukuk-al-ijara* primarily due to its simplicity and acceptance across all Islamic schools of thought.

The term *'ijara'* is broadly means the 'transfer of the use of an asset to another person in exchange for a rent claimed' or, more literally, a 'lease'. For those accustomed to conventional terminology, an *ijara* is a hybrid between an operating lease and a finance lease.

An example of a *sukuk-al-ijara* structure, based upon a sale and leaseback approach is set out in Figure 4.2 on page 55.

4.2.1. Overview of Sukuk-al-ijara Structure: On the Issuance Date

(Using the numbering from Figure 4.2 on page 55)

(1a) The Issuer SPV issues sukuk, which for international transactions will be way of declaration of trust. The Issuer SPV, once the trust has been declared, will be acting as Issuer and Trustee and will hold all its assets and rights from time to time on trust for the investors. The sukuk provides an investor with a right against Issuer SPV to certain payments, namely the economic return on the sukuk (which is often referred to as the coupon or the periodic distribution amount) and the return of capital (which is often referred to as the redemption amount or dissolution amount).

(1b) The investors subscribe for sukuk and pay the proceeds to Issuer (the Issuance Proceeds). The Issuer SPV declares a trust over the Issuance Proceeds (and any assets acquired using the Issuance Proceeds) and thereby acts as Trustee on behalf of the investors. For those of you familiar with the common law concepts of a trust, the Issuer SPV is therefore both the settlor and issuer of the trust.

(2a) The Obligor enters into a sale and purchase arrangement with Issuer SPV, pursuant to which Obligor sells, and Issuer SPV will purchase, certain identified assets (the Sukuk Assets) from the Obligor. The term sale is used as a generic concept as the manner of the sale will depend upon the asset itself and it is not uncommon to refer to the sale as a sale, transfer or conveyance. These Sukuk Assets must however be physical assets that are capable of being used – so they cannot be intangible assets but can be moveable assets such as plant and machinery or can be immoveable assets such as real estate.

Once the Obligor has received the sale proceeds it is free to use those proceeds in any way it deems appropriate, assuming that is of course sharia compliant. There are no use of proceeds restrictions tied to this structure.

There is often a debate as to whether this sale, transfer needs to be perfected or not – this is not a question with a simple answer as it will vary from jurisdiction to jurisdiction and will dependent upon the legal and tax analysis. The starting points is that from an Islamic perspective all that is required for the Issuer SPV to acquire an ownership interest is the entry into of a sale and purchase agreement. However the legal and tax analysis of where the assets are located also needs to be examined and whether the sale agreement alone will be recognised as creating an interest in the asset in favour of the Issuer SPV. The market practice that has developed unfortunately is not uniform but in all cases is essentially ensuring at making sure that the Issuer SPV and the Obligor do not become exposed to additional tax liabilities given that, on asset based structures, the commercial intention is to replicate the economics of a conventional senior unsecured bond.

To give you a few examples:

- In Saudi Arabia, where the laws are all based on the principles of sharia, the execution of the sale agreement alone would be sufficient to give the Issuer SPV an ownership interest.

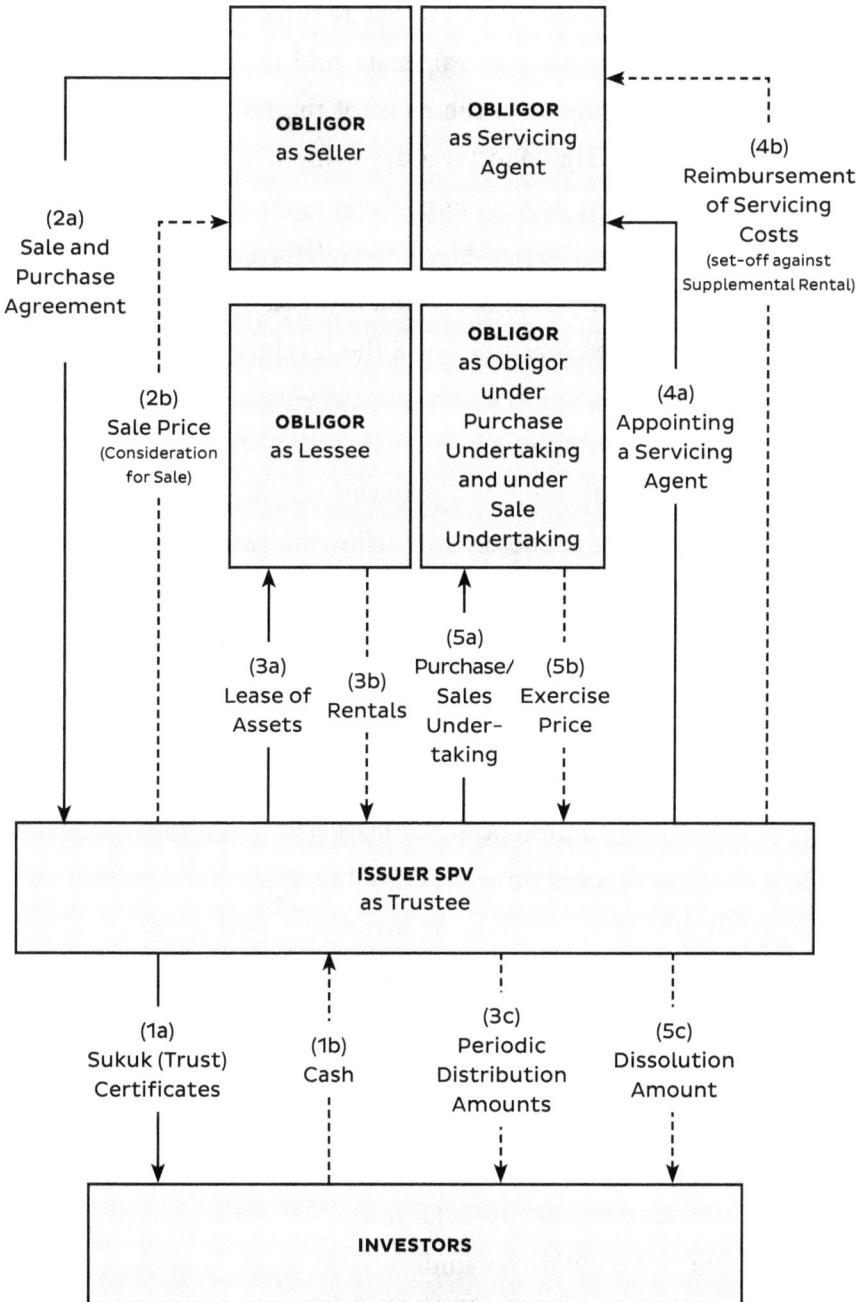

OBLIGOR
as Seller

OBLIGOR
as Servicing
Agent

(4b)
Reimbursement
of Servicing
Costs
(set-off against
Supplemental Rental)

(2a)
Sale and
Purchase
Agreement

OBLIGOR
as Lessee

OBLIGOR
as Obligor
under
Purchase
Undertaking
and under
Sale
Undertaking

(2b)
Sale Price
(Consideration
for Sale)

(4a)
Appointing
a Servicing
Agent

(3a)
Lease of
Assets

(3b)
Rentals

(5a)
Purchase/
Sales
Under-
taking

(5b)
Exercise
Price

ISSUER SPV
as Trustee

(1a)
Sukuk (Trust)
Certificates

(1b)
Cash

(3c)
Periodic
Distribution
Amounts

(5c)
Dissolution
Amount

INVESTORS

KEY | ———— Agreement / Documents | - - - - - - - Cash Flow

Figure 4.2: Structure of Sukuk-al-ijara

- In the UK, the tax and real estate rules are sufficiently well developed that the real estate sold to the Issuer SPV has to be registered in the name of the Issuer SPV and, provided certain conditions are complied with as set out in the relevant provisions of the Finance Act, no stamp duty or SDLT will be payable on the sale, so essentially ensuring the tax analysis of the sukuk is the same as a conventional bond. Therefore to ensure the level playing field from a tax perspective, the sale must be registered creating a legal ownership interest in the name of the Issuer SPV.

- In the UAE, the sale agreement would not be recognised as part of a financing transaction but rather as a real estate transaction and therefore, for the sale agreement to be effective and enforceable at law, the sale agreement must be registered and the relevant lands department registration fees (equivalent of stamp duty) paid. However given that this is contrary to the commercial intention that this is a financing transaction, the market has developed a 'work around' based on complicated analysis of restitution and indemnity provisions to ensure investors are not exposed to additional risks as relative to a bond (or those risks are at least mitigated). This complicated work around is premised on the enforceability of English law indemnities and restitution provisions in the courts of the ADGM and the DIFC which would give effect to English law principles. Whilst this legal complexity is far from ideal, at the time of writing, there are initiatives underway to ensure a sale agreement entered into as part of a sukuk transaction should be recognised as a financing transaction thereby seeking to remove the unnecessary legal complexity and risk.

- In Turkey, Malaysia and Indonesia the analysis is similar to the UK (although there are slight variances which are jurisdictionally driven).

The general rule, however, is that all steps need to be taken to ensure that the sale agreement is a legally enforceable contract, such as registration, unless there is a commercial rationale for not doing so (e.g. payment of taxes and fees), provided such non-registration does not prejudice the rights of the investors.

(2b) The Issuer SPV pays the purchase price to Obligor as consideration for its purchase of the Sukuk Assets in an amount equal to the Issuance Proceeds. The value ascribed to the Sukuk Asset is the market value of the Sukuk Asset in the reasonable determination of the Obligor. Most Obligors will of course have a value ascribed to the asset which is the value given to it in its financial statements. This is a key point to note, namely the issuance amount of any *sukuk-al-ijara* is limited by the value of the assets.

(3a) The Issuer SPV leases the Sukuk Assets to Obligor under a lease arrangement referred to as an *ijara* agreement for a term that reflects the maturity of the sukuk. So if the sukuk is issued for a tenor of five years, then the lease agreement will also have a tenor of five years.

4.2.2. Overview of Sukuk–al–ijara Structure: Post Issuance

(Using the numbering from Figure 4.2 on page 55)

(3b) The Obligor (in its capacity as lessee) will make rental payments at regular intervals to Issuer SPV (in its capacity as lessor). The amount of each rental payment is equal to the periodic distribution amount payable under the sukuk by the Issuer SPV to the investors at that time. This amount may be calculated by reference to a fixed rate or variable rate (e.g. a benchmark rate) depending on the commercial intention of the parties at the outset.

(3c) The Issuer SPV pays each periodic distribution amount to the investors using the rental it has received from Obligor.

(4a & 4b) The Issuer SPV and Obligor enter into a service agency agreement whereby Issuer SPV will appoint Obligor as its Servicing Agent to carry out certain of its obligations under the lease arrangement, namely the obligation to undertake any major maintenance, the obligation to maintain insurance (or takaful) and payment of taxes in connection with the Sukuk Assets. To the extent that Obligor (as Servicing Agent) claims any costs and expenses for performing these obligations (the Servicing Costs) the rental for the subsequent lease period under the lease arrangement will be increased by an equivalent amount (a Supplemental Rental). This Supplemental Rental due from Obligor (as Lessee) will be set off against the obligation of Issuer SPV to pay the Servicing Costs. (In the last few months however this position has evolved in certain markets driven by sharia concerns that it is unconsidered unfair to contractually demand that the Obligor (in its capacity) as lessee be obliged to pay Supplementary Rent simply because the Obligor (in its capacity as Servicing Agent) has claimed Servicing Costs. Whilst the economics of the sukuk remain the same given the commercial intention is to have a senior unsecured fixed income instrument, the methodology and approach has changed slightly so that the Servicing Agent is put into funds to perform such servicing/maintenance at the time of issuance from the issuance proceeds. Please see Chapter 6 (*Recent Developments*) for more information.

4.2.3. Overview of Sukuk-al-ijara Structure: Early/Scheduled Dissolution

(Using the numbering from Figure 4.2 on page 55)

(5a & 5b) Upon maturity/scheduled dissolution date or upon the occurrence of an agreed default/dissolution event, the Issuer SPV (and therefore the Delegate) has the right to sell the Sukuk Assets back to the Obligor. This right is exercised by the Issuer SPV (or the Delegate on its behalf) exercising the purchase undertaking. The purchase undertaking is similar to a put option that has been entered into at the outset of the transaction and once exercised by the Issuer SPV/Delegate, the Obligor becomes obliged to pay the pre-agreed exercise price. The exercise price is the amount required to redeem the sukuk certificates in full so will be equal to the unpaid periodic distribution amount and the redemption amount. On a senior unsecured deal, in the event the Obligor fails to pay, the investors will only have a debt claim against the Obligor for the unpaid exercise price. It is important to note that this purchase undertaking is a unilateral right granted by the Obligor in favour of the Issuer SPV.

The transaction will also include a sale undertaking which is equivalent of a call option. The sale undertaking can be exercised if, due to a change in tax legislation, the cost of the sukuk financing becomes more expensive than at the outset of the transaction (e.g. a change in the withholding tax rules), or, where commercially agreed, can include an optional call i.e. a right to voluntarily prepay which may be used where for example the sukuk has become an expensive form of financing. In the case of the latter this essentially means that the Obligor has the right to buy the Sukuk Assets back and prepay the sukuk. There is of course a commercial implication on the coupon amount to include an optional call into a fixed income instrument such as a sukuk.

(5c) Issuer SPV pays the Dissolution Amount to the investors using the exercise price it has received from Obligor.

4.2.4. Key Features of the Ijara Structure

Whilst there are come core principles of an *ijara* structure that will be adopted for every transaction, certain elements will vary depending on which jurisdiction the Obligor is located, the identity of the lead banks and who the sharia scholar is. Whilst this does lead to some divergence there are some fundamental principles that will apply to all sukuk-al-ijara regardless of any of the above:

- The subject matter of the *ijara* agreement must be capable of being used and anything which can be consumed cannot be leased by way of an *ijara*.

- Ownership (or another right equivalent to ownership) of the asset(s) must remain with the Issuer SPV, the liabilities arising from the ownership must also rest with the Issuer SPV (as owner) – the asset remains the risk of the Issuer SPV throughout the lease period (in the sense that any harm or loss caused by the factors beyond the control of the Obligor is borne by the Issuer SPV).

- Any liabilities relating to the use of the asset(s), however, rest with the Obligor (as lessee).

- The Obligor (as lessee) cannot use the asset for any purpose other than the purpose specified in the *ijara* (or lease) agreement (if no purpose is specified, the Obligor can use such asset for the purpose it would be used for in the normal course of its business).

- The asset(s) must be clearly identified in the *ijara* (and identifiable in practice).

- Rental must be determined at the time of commencement for the whole period of the *ijara*. Although it is possible to split the term of the *ijara* into smaller rental periods where different amounts of rent may be calculated for each such rental period, the amount of rental must be fixed at the start of each such rental period and sharia will consider each rental period as a separate lease.

- If an asset has totally lost the function for which it was leased, and no repair is possible, the *ijara* shall terminate on the day on which such loss (a Total Loss) has been caused. If there has been a Total Loss, the Issuer SPV may have the right/ability to substitute or replace the affected asset – although, in reality, it would only look to do so if the Obligor (as service agent) is able to use the insurance (or *takaful*) or any other total loss proceeds to procure substitute or replacement assets.

- If a Total Loss is caused by the misuse or negligence of the Obligor, the Obligor will be liable to compensate the Issuer SPV for depreciation in the value of the affected asset, as it was immediately before such Total Loss.

- In the event that an asset has only suffered partial loss or damage, the *ijara* will continue to survive with respect to that asset. However, please see Chapter 6 (*Recent Developments*) for further details in connection with HSA/AAOIFI requirements in the UAE.

The above requirements are based on the principles set out in Accounting and Auditing Organisation for Islamic Financial Institutions (AAOIFI) Sharia Standard No. 9 (*Ijarah and Ijarah Muntahia Bittamleek*) and other established principles relating to *ijara*.

4.2.5. Required Islamic Documentation for Sukuk–al–ijara

The following Islamic documentation is typically required for a *sukuk-al-ijara* transaction:

DOCUMENT	PARTIES	SUMMARY / PURPOSE
Sale and Purchase Agreement	Obligor (as Seller) and Issuer SPV (as Purchaser)	From Issuer SPV's (and the investors') perspective, this is the document that gives the Issuer SPV ownership of revenue-generating assets (i.e. the Sukuk Assets). From Obligor's perspective, this is the document under which it receives funding
Lease (*Ijara*) Agreement	Issuer SPV (as Lessor) and Obligor (as Lessee)	Issuer SPV leases the Sukuk Assets back to Obligor in a manner that gives Obligor possession and use of the Sukuk Assets so that its principal business can continue without interruption. By payment of lease rentals it generates a return for Issuer SPV (and the investors)
Service Agency Agreement	Issuer SPV (as Lessor / Principal) and Obligor (as Servicing Agent)	Allows Issuer SPV to pass responsibility for major maintenance, insurance (or *takaful*) and payment of taxes (i.e. an owner's obligations) back to Obligor. Any reimbursement amounts or service charges payable to Servicing Agent are set off against (i) a corresponding 'supplementary rental' under the *ijara* or (ii) an additional amount which is added to the Exercise Price (payable under the Purchase Undertaking or the Sale Undertaking, as applicable). See Chapter 6 (*Recent Developments*)

DOCUMENT	PARTIES	SUMMARY / PURPOSE
Purchase Undertaking (*Wa'ad*)	Granted by Obligor (as Obligor) in favour of Issuer SPV	Allows Issuer SPV to sell the Sukuk Assets back to Obligor if an event of default/dissolution occurs or at maturity, in return for which Obligor is required to pay all outstanding amounts (through an Exercise Price) so that Issuer SPV can pay the investors
Sale Undertaking (*Wa'ad*)	Granted by Issuer SPV in favour of Obligor (as Obligor)	Allows Obligor to buy the Sukuk Assets back from Issuer SPV in limited circumstances (e.g. the occurrence of a tax event), in return for which Obligor is required to pay all outstanding amounts (through an Exercise Price) so that Issuer SPV can pay the investors
Substitution Undertaking (*Wa'ad*)	Granted by Issuer SPV in favour of Obligor (as Obligor)	Allows Obligor to substitute the Sukuk Assets (which it may need to sell or otherwise dispose of) for other assets having at least the same value and revenue-generating properties. Sometimes the substitution undertaking is built into the sale undertaking, so there is a sale and substitution undertaking

4.2.6. Required Capital Market Documentation for Sukuk-al-ijara

The following underlying capital market documentation is typically required for a *sukuk-al-ijara* transaction:

DOCUMENT	PARTIES	SUMMARY / PURPOSE
Prospectus (including terms & conditions)		The Prospectus will set out key risk factors, disclosure on the Obligor and Issuer SPV as well as key other information that investors need to be aware of as part of making an informed investment decision

Declaration of Trust	Issuer SPV, Obligor and Delegate	Creation of the trust certificates and appointment of Delegate and empowering delegate to take certain actions under certain circumstances e.g. Obligor default
Agency Agreement	Issuer SPV, Obligor, Delegate, Paying Agent, Transfer Agent, Calculation Agent	Appointment of Agents
Subscription Agreement	Issuer SPV, Obligor, Joint Lead Managers	Subscription of the Sukuk by the Joint Lead Managers

4.2.7. Related Structures / Structural Developments for Sukuk-al-ijara

The growth of the *sukuk* market has led to the development of some flexibility for *sukuk-al-ijara*, particularly when selecting underlying assets. A few of these developments are summarised below:

- In order to enable investors to receive compensation where an asset is still under construction, certain sharia scholars have permitted the use of the forward lease arrangement (known as *ijara mawsufah fi al-dimmah*). This forward lease agreement is normally combined with an *istisna* contract (or procurement agreement), under which construction of the asset is commissioned. This structure is discussed in detail at Part 4.5.6 (*Sukuk-al-istisna*) of this chapter.

- If legal and/or registered title to a particular asset exists and (due to, by way of example, the prohibitive cost implications or tax implications of registering such a transfer of title) it is not possible to transfer that legal / registered title, certain structures have been approved that allow an *ijara* to be put in place despite the fact that the trustee does not have outright legal ownership of that asset. For example:

1   It may be possible, depending on the asset type and the view taken by the relevant sharia scholars, to rely upon the concept of beneficial ownership in structuring a *sukuk-al-ijara* transaction. The sale and purchase agreement (in the sale and leaseback structure discussed above) would document the sale and transfer to the Issuer SPV of the beneficial ownership interest in the underlying asset, and such beneficial ownership interest would be sufficient to enable the Issuer SPV's entry into the leaseback arrangements contemplated in the example above;

2   Where the usufruct of an asset is recognised by the underlying legal and regulatory regime, it may be possible for the sale of a usufruct to be relied upon for the purposes of structuring a *sukuk-al-ijara* transaction. A usufruct provides an interest less than freehold or absolute ownership. The usufruct right, when created, is granted by the owner of the freehold property to the holder. The right, while not a leasehold interest, is a right 'in rem' and is therefore considered similar to ownership. Certain sharia scholars consider this sufficient to enable the usufruct holder, in turn, to lease the land and any buildings thereon to the obligor under an *ijara* arrangement; and

3   It is also possible for a head-lease arrangement to be used instead of the sale and purchase agreement (in the sale and leaseback structure discussed above), such that the Issuer SPV is granted a long-term right to use an asset under the head-lease, thus allowing the Issuer SPV to enter into a sub-lease (the *ijara*).

4.3. Sukuk-al-murabaha

The term *murabaha* refers to a contractual arrangement between one party (the seller) and another party (the purchaser) whereby the seller sells specified assets or commodities for spot delivery, and usually in financial transactions, for deferred payment. The deferred payment price would typically consist of the cost price at which the seller had purchased the assets/commodities, plus a pre-agreed mark-up representing the profit generated from its involvement in the transaction. The payments of the deferred price from the buyer may be structured as periodic/instalment payments or a bullet payment.

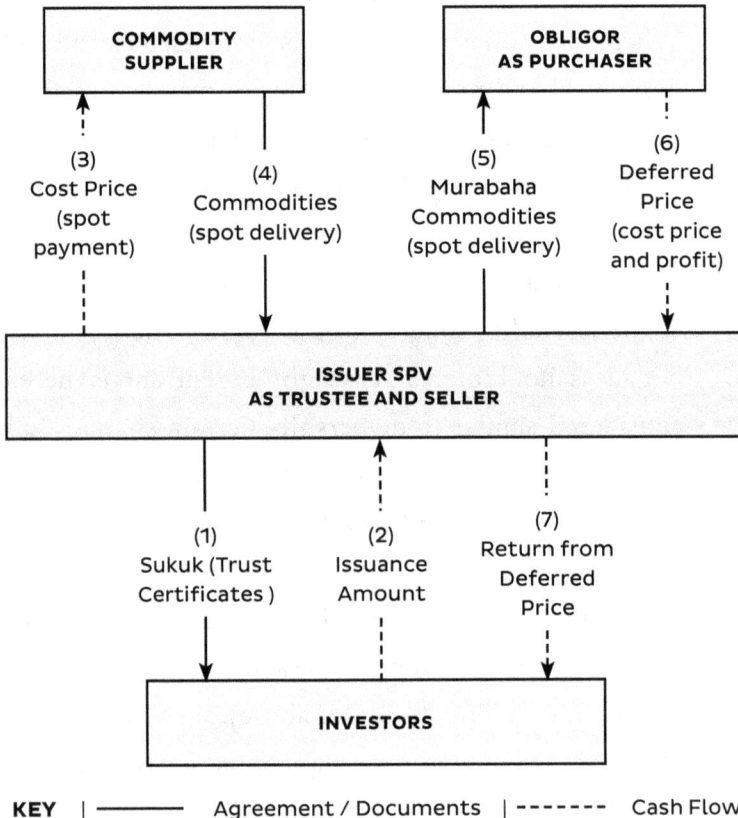

Figure 4.3: Structure of Sukuk-al-murabaha

These characteristics of the *murabaha* structure can also be adapted for use as the underlying structure in a *sukuk* issuance. However this does come with some caution and is certainly not globally accepted. I will discuss the reasons why but let us look at how a *sukuk-al-murabaha* can be structured.

Set out below is an example of a typical *sukuk-al-murabaha* structure.

4.3.1. Overview of Sukuk-al-murabaha Structure

(Using the numbering from Figure 4.3 on page 66)

(1) The Issuer SPV issues sukuk, which for international transactions will be way of declaration of trust. The Issuer SPV, once the trust has been declared, will be acting as Issuer and Trustee will hold all its assets and rights from time to time on trust for the investors. The sukuk provides an investor with a right against Issuer SPV to certain payments, namely the economic return on the sukuk (which is often referred to as the coupon or the periodic distribution amount) and the return of capital (which is often referred to as the redemption amount or dissolution amount).

(2) The investors subscribe for sukuk and pay the proceeds to Issuer SPV (the Issuance Amount). The Issuer SPV declares a trust over the Issuance Amount (and any investment made using the Issuance Amount) and thereby acts as Trustee on behalf of the investors. For those of you familiar with the common law concepts of a trust, the Issuer SPV is therefore both the settlor and issuer of the trust.

(5) The Obligor (as Purchaser) enters into a *murabaha* agreement with Issuer SPV (as Seller), pursuant to which Issuer SPV agrees to sell, and Obligor agrees to purchase, certain sharia compliant commodities (the Commodities) from Issuer SPV on spot delivery

and deferred payment terms. The actual individual sale is often referred to as a *murabaha* contract (which is entered into under the terms of the *murabaha* agreement). The period for the payment of the deferred price will reflect the maturity of the sukuk. The actual entry into of the *murabaha* contract (i.e. the specific sale under the *murabaha* agreement) utilises the following structure:

i   The Obligor will notify the Seller that it wishes to purchase from it certain identified sharia compliant commodities for a specific cost amount. This notification is usually called a 'Notice of Intent to Purchase'. In this notice the Obligor will also undertake that if the Issuer SPV purchases the required Commodities, then once the Issuer SPV is in a position to sell them to the Purchaser, the Purchaser undertakes that it will buy them. This is not a forward sale but is simply of an undertaking or promise to purchase in due course.

ii   The Issuer SPV will then use the Issuance Amount to purchase the required Commodities from a third party referred to as the 'Commodity Supplier' (steps 3 and 4 in Figure 4.3). The identity of the third party can vary – in certain jurisdictions the purchase will be done in what is known as 'OTC' or 'over the counter'. In other words the sale does not involve a commodities exchange. In certain other jurisdictions the Issuer SPV may purchase the commodities 'on-exchange'. Once the Issuer SPV has purchased the commodities from the Commodity Supplier it will then issue an offer notice to the Purchaser offering to sell the Commodities. The offer notice will include the required detail including the exact details of the Commodities, their location, the cost price and the proposed profit amount. The profit amount is calculated on the basis of the coupon amount payable to the investors under the Sukuk. So for example, if the Sukuk issuance amount is USD 100 with a coupon amount of 5 per cent per annum with a 5-year maturity, the profit on the *murabaha* contract will be USD 25.

iii The Obligor as purchaser will accept the offer by issuing an acceptance notice. At this point the Obligor will become the legal owner of the Commodities and will have a deferred payment obligation to the Issuer SPV.

An an aside it is worth noting that there is a further leg to the transaction which sits outside of the Sukuk. Based on the fact pattern above the Obligor will at the end of the transaction have legal title to the Commodities. However the Obligor will actually want the issuance proceeds as cash for its general business. The Obligor will therefore enter into an on-sale agreement with a different third party (referred to as the Commodity Purchaser) whereby the Obligor will sell the purchased Commodities to the Commodity Purchaser for spot delivery and also spot payment.

As a consequence of this the Obligor now has funds which it can use for its general business and a deferred payment obligation to the Trustee/SPV.

4.3.2. Key Features of the Murabaha Structure

Set out below is a summary of the basic requirements which should be considered when using *murabaha* as the underlying structure for the issuance of *sukuk*:

- The deferred purchase price must be at an agreed rate and for an agreed period.
- In order to ensure that Issuer SPV obtains marketable title to the Commodities from Commodity Supplier to facilitate their

on-sale to Obligor, Issuer SPV may require certain representations and warranties from the Commodity Suppler that the Commodities will be sold free of any encumbrances or liens.

- During the period of ownership of the Commodities by Issuer SPV, there is a risk of price fluctuation in the market value of the Commodities which can be mitigated by minimising the duration of Issuer SPV's ownership which is usually limited to intra-day.

- If Obligor requests physical delivery (as opposed to constructive delivery), there may be a risk that the Commodities are damaged whilst in transit which may be mitigated by undertakings from Obligor in the *murabaha* agreement to accept the Commodities on an "as is" basis.

- Depending on the type of Commodities involved, and the jurisdiction of the parties, tax liabilities in respect of the acquisition and sale of the Commodities should be considered in order to maximise the preservation of the principal amount in the Cost Price.

4.3.3. Required Islamic Documentation for Sukuk-al-murabaha

DOCUMENT	PARTIES	SUMMARY / PURPOSE
Murabaha Agreement	Obligor (as Purchaser) and Issuer SPV (as Seller)	Issuer SPV (and the investor) sells Commodities to Obligor on spot delivery and deferred payment terms. Documents the terms of the *murabaha* sale transaction as well as terms of payment of deferred price
Sale and Purchase Agreement	Issuer SPV (as Buyer) and Commodity Supplier (as Supplier)	Commodity Supplier sells Commodities to Trustee on spot delivery and spot payment terms

4.3.4. Required Capital Market Documentation for Sukuk-al-murabaha

DOCUMENT	PARTIES	SUMMARY / PURPOSE
Prospectus (including terms & conditions)		The Prospectus will set out key risk factors, disclosure on the Obligor and Issuer SPV as well as key other information that investors need to be aware of as part of making an informed investment decision
Declaration of Trust	Issuer SPV, Obligor and Delegate	Creation of the trust certificates and appointment of Delegate and empowerting delegate to take certain actions under certain circumstances e.g. Obligor default
Agency Agreement	Issuer SPV, Obligor, Delegate, Paying Agent, Transfer Agent, Calculation Agent	Appointment of Agents
Subscription Agreement	Trustee, Obligor, Joint Lead Managers	Subscription of the Sukuk by the Joint Lead Managers

4.3.5. Related Structures/Structural Developments for Sukuk-al-murabaha

As mentioned above, the issuance of a *sukuk-al-murabaha* gives rise to sharia concerns in certain jurisdiction.

In a *murabaha* sukuk where the Issuer SPV is the seller, once the seller has sold the commodities to the buyer (the Obligor), the seller does not own any physical or tangible assets. It only has a receivable, which is the right to receive the deferred purchase price from the Obligor. Under the rules of Islamic jurisprudence as applied in certain parts of the world, principally the Middle East, a receivable is classified as a debt and a debt can only be transferred at par value. It cannot be transferred at any kind of discount or premium. Therefore, from an investor perspective, any *sukuk-al-murabaha* is essentially an instrument that has to be held to maturity.

As a result of this in certain jurisdictions such as the UAE, any regulated investor (as regulated by the UAE Central Bank) is no longer able to participate in the arrangement, sale or purchase of *sukuk-al-murabaha*. In addition, existing *murabaha* receivables may not be sold at anything other than par value and *murabaha* receivables themselves may not form part of the subject matter of a further sukuk issuance.

As a consequence of these developments the volume of *sukuk-al-murabaha* has, in certain parts of the world, decreased significantly. It is worth noting that *sukuk-al-murabaha* has not been removed completely but is still issued in other GCC jurisdictions (with the limitation that the investor cannot trade at other than par) and also issued in certain South East jurisdictions such as Malaysia (where there are no limitations on the value ascribed to the receivable when it is sold in the secondary market so can be sold at a premium or a discount).

Finally, it is worth noting that *murabaha* can still form a component part of a wider sukuk issuance. This will be examined in more detail in the next section.

4.4. Sukuk-al-wakala

The concept of a *wakala* is an arrangement where one party appoints another party to act as agent on its behalf, either on a disclosed or an undisclosed basis.

A principal (the *muwakkil*) appoints an agent (*wakeel*) to invest funds provided by the principal into a single asset/investment or into a pool of investments/assets and the *wakeel* provides its expertise and manages those investments on behalf of the principal for a particular duration, in order to generate an agreed upon profit return. The principal and *wakeel* enter into a *wakala* agreement, which will govern the appointment, scope of services and fees payable to the *wakeel*. The relationship between the principal and the *wakeel* must comply with certain basic conditions, which are described below in "Key Features of *Sukuk-al-wakala*".

To the extent the *wakeel* has discretion on how to manage the funds then the *wakala* arrangement is referred to as an investment *wakala*. To the extent there is no discretion and the *wakeel* is instructed to purchase certain assets and manage them in a particular way, then this is a management/service *wakala*. There is a key difference between the two which means that for a management/service *wakala*, it is possible to use a fixed price purchase undertaking but for an investment *wakala*, it is not.

The *wakala* structure is particularly useful where the underlying assets available to the Obligor, and which can be used to support the issuance of the *sukuk*, comprise a pool or portfolio of assets or investments as opposed to a particular tangible asset or assets. The *wakeel* thereby uses its expertise to select and manage investments on behalf of the investor to ensure that the portfolio will generate the expected profit rate agreed by the principal. While the *wakala* structure has some similarities with the *mudaraba* structure, the main differences are:

1   The mudaraba is a relationship between two principals whilst a *wakala* is a relationship between a principal and its agent.

2   In a mudaraba arrangement all profit generated is divided between the parties according to certain ratios. In a *wakala* structure the *muwakkil* will receive all the profit return agreed between the parties at the outset. The *wakeel* will be paid a

nominal fee and only any profit in excess of the agreed upon profit return will be kept by the *wakeel* as a performance or an incentive fee.

From a strict sharia compliant perspective, the assets purchased/invested in by a *wakeel* can be any sharia compliant asset including equities (which are issued by companies complying with certain sharia guidelines or listed on sharia approved indices), other sharia compliant assets (such as *murabaha, istisna* or even other sukuk – see below), provided they meet sharia guidelines.

However in the context of a *wakala* sukuk which has a fixed price purchase undertaking, the assets which can be included in the portfolio of *wakala* assets cannot now include equities or receivables. Receivables cannot be included due to the prohibition of purchasing debt for other than par (and as discussed in Part 4.3, *Sukuk-al-murabaha*, of this chapter). Equities cannot be included and the reasons for this are discussed further below. Further information is included on this in Chapter 6 (*Recent Developments*).

In recent years there has been a significant development where the *wakala* includes a *murabaha* component – so in other words the Issuer SPV issuance (which is the *muwakkil*) may use a portion of the issuance proceeds to enter into a commodity *murabaha*. The advantage of this is that it allows an Obligor to leverage its asset base, or in other words increase the size of any issuance beyond the physical assets available on its balance sheet. This structure is often referred to a hybrid *wakala-murabaha* structure and has become the structure of choice when sukuk are being issued by Islamic banks or Islamic financial institutions. In fact virtually every financial institution in the GCC that has issued a USD sukuk

in the last few years has used this structure. The structure is however not without some academic debate and has been approved
on the basis of certain parameters namely that:

- The tangibility of the *wakala-murabaha* cannot ever be lower
  than 51 per cent. In other words, the sukuk assets owned by
  the *wakeel* must be at least 51 per cent tangible at all times,
  including after the commodity transaction has been entered
  into between the Issuer SPV and the Obligor. There are consequences which flow from a breach of the tangibility ratio.
  See Chapter 6 (*Recent Developments*) for more information.

- Ideally the issuance has to be a fixed rate series. However if a
  floating rate series is opted for then the *murabaha* component has
  to be always fixed in any event and the floating rate can only be
  structured through the *wakala* component excluding the *murabaha*. This adds a layer of structural and drafting complexity.

4.4.1. Overview of Sukuk-al-wakala Structure

(using the numbering from Figure 4.4 on page 76):

(1) The Issuer SPV issues *sukuk,* which for international transactions will be way of declaration of trust. The Issuer SPV,
once the trust has been declared, will be acting as Issuer and
Trustee will hold all its assets and rights from time to time on
trust for the investors. The sukuk provides an investor with a
right against Issuer to certain payments, namely the economic
return on the sukuk (which is often referred to as the coupon
or the periodic distribution amount) and the return of capital
(which is often referred to as the redemption amount or dissolution amount).

(2) The investors subscribe for sukuk and pay the proceeds to
Issuer (the Issuance Amount). The Issuer SPV declares a trust

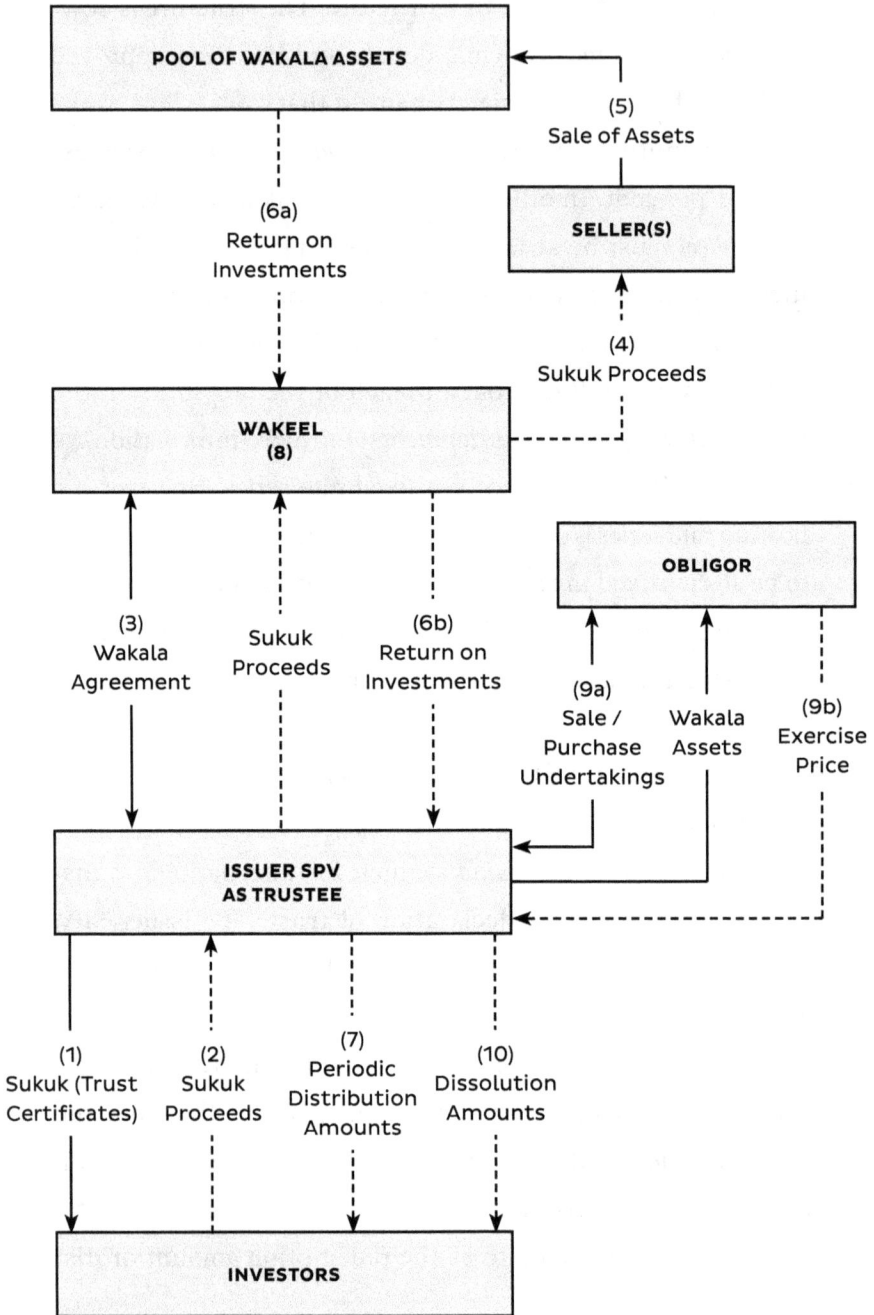

Figure 4.4: Structure of Sukuk-al-wakala

over the proceeds (and any investment made using the proceeds) and thereby acts as Trustee on behalf of the investors. For those of you familiar with the common law concepts of a trust, the Issuer SPV is therefore both the settlor and issuer of the trust.

(3) The Issuer SPV, in its capacity as principal, enters into a *wakala* agreement with the Obligor as *wakeel*. The *wakeel* agrees to invest the *sukuk* proceeds, on behalf of the Issuer SPV, in a pool or portfolio of investments (the *wakala* assets), selected by the *wakeel*, in accordance with specified criteria.

(4) The *sukuk proceeds* will be used by the *wakeel* to purchase the selected *wakala* assets. These may be purchased from the Obligor in its role as a seller. The *wakala* assets cannot include intangible asset or receivables.

(5) The *wakala* assets will be held and managed by the *wakeel*, on behalf of the Issuer SPV, for the duration of the *sukuk* in order to generate an expected profit. The *wakala* assets will constitute part of the trust assets held by the Issuer SPV (in its capacity as trustee) on behalf of the investors.

(6a & 6b) The *wakala* assets will generate a profit return, which will be held by the *wakeel* on behalf of the Issuer SPV. This income generated will be recorded by the *wakeel* in a ledger account referred to as the 'Collection Account'. A ledger account is a book entry of the *wakeel* and not a physical separate account.

(7) The profit return will be used to fund the periodic distribution amounts payable by the Issuer SPV to the investors. Any profit in excess of the periodic distribution amounts on any periodic distribution date will be paid debited from the Collection Account and will be credited to a further ledger account known as the 'Reserve Account'. Again this is a book entry account maintained by the *wakeel*. The periodic

distribution amounts – either a fixed or variable amount calculated as per a fixed formula – will be paid to the investors on the relevant periodic distribution dates.

(8) Any funds standing to the credit of the Reserve Account may be withdrawn and used by the *wakeel* for its own purposes provided that if there is any shortfall on any future periodic distribution date then this amount must be refunded/recredited by the *wakeel*. Any amounts remaining in the Reserve Account once the sukuk has been redeemed may be retained by the *wakeel* as an incentive fee. It is possible that the *wakala* assets in any particular period may generate a return that is less than the required periodic distribution amount.

There are various mitigants against this as follows:

• As mentioned above any income or profit generated by the *wakeel* will be deposited into an 'Collection Account'. On each periodic distribution date any profit up to the periodic distribution amount will be paid to investors but any profit in excess of the required periodic distribution amount on that date will be transferred into a 'Reserve Account'. If on any future periodic distribution dates the profit generated is less than the periodic distribution amount then due, funds sitting to the credit of the 'Reserve Account' can be used to make up any shortfall.

• In the event there are insufficient funds in the Reserve Account then the *wakeel* may procure from a third party or provide from its own resources a sharia compliant liquidity facility equal to any shortfall. This liquidity facility must be repaid from any future excess income from the *wakala* assets or must be repaid by the exercise price under the purchase undertaking being increased by an equivalent amount.

(9a & 9b) Upon:

    i   the maturity date or upon the occurrence of an event of default (i.e. dissolution event), the Issuer SPV will exercise its option under the Purchase Undertaking to require the Obligor to purchase the *wakala* assets at an Exercise Price that is equal to the dissolution amount payable to investors together with any accrued but unpaid periodic distribution amounts.

    ii   the exercise of an optional call (if applicable) or the occurrence of a tax event, the Obligor will exercise its option under the sale undertaking to buy the *wakala* assets from the Issuer SPV at an Exercise Price that is equal to the Dissolution Amount payable to investors together with any accrued but unpaid periodic distribution amounts.

(10) Upon the occurrence of one of the events described in (9) above, the Issuer SPV will pay the dissolution amount to investors using the Exercise Price received from investors and redeem the *sukuk*, upon which the trust will be dissolved.

4.4.2. Key Features of the Wakala Structure

Some of the basic requirements that should be considered when using *wakala* as the underlying structure of the issuance of *sukuk* are:

- The scope of the *wakala* arrangement must be within the boundaries of sharia i.e. the principal/Issuer SPV cannot require the *wakeel* to perform tasks that would not otherwise be sharia compliant.

- The subject matter of the *wakala* arrangement must be clear and unambiguous and must be set out in the *wakala* agreement i.e. the duration of the *wakala*, the type or criteria of assets that the *wakeel* can select, the fees payable to the *wakeel* for its services and the conditions for termination of the *wakala* agreement.

- The principal (the Issuer SPV) can only receive the expected profit, i.e. the amount used to fund the Periodic Distribution Amounts. Any excess will be held by the *wakeel* for its benefit.

- The *wakala* assets must comply with any agreed eligibility criteria. Additionally at least 51 per cent of the portfolio of assets should comprise tangible assets (such as *ijara* assets or *ijara* sukuk). The Obligor must therefore assess whether it has a sufficient quantity of the relevant assets to satisfy this ratio. It is worth noting that this is minimum tangibility ratio has historically varied between 33 and 51 per cent, and often sukuk have permitted fluctuations between the two. However the current position as recommended by AAOIFI and almost universally adopted on all transactions is that the minimum tangibility cannot be below 51 per cent on the issuance date of the transaction.

- In addition, a sharia board would typically impose further criteria, which may include (but not be limited to) the following:

  i   If the pool comprises equities, the *wakeel* may only purchase equities of companies where the primary business activity of the company is compliant with sharia. Most scholars however do not allow the use of equities in fixed price *wakala* sukuk – the rationale being that the value of a share inherently represents the underlying value of the company by which they are issued and therefore to trade them at a price other than that is not sharia compliant; and

ii   If the pool comprises *sukuk*, the *sukuk* must have been approved by the relevant sharia board and must be fully backed by tangible assets.

• If, any of the assets cease to be sharia compliant at any time during the duration of the sukuk, they must be removed from the pool of assets and be replaced with sharia-compliant assets. There must therefore be a mechanism for substituting assets. This may be achieved through the purchase undertaking or a separate substitution undertaking whereby the Obligor may be required to purchase the non-compliant asset from the pool in consideration for a new sharia-compliant asset.

To the extent a commodity *murabaha* component is added it is important to ensure that the deferred payment price of the commodity *murabaha* cannot exceed 49 per cent of the issuance amount. This means that a lower percentage than 49 per cent must be used as the cost price component of the *murabaha* and once the profit component is added in then the deferred purchase price will not exceed 49 per cent.

So, for example, if a sukuk is to pay 5 per cent coupon then a portion of that coupon amount must come from the profit on the *murabaha* component and a portion of that 5 per cent must come from the *wakala* assets. Whilst there is no firm rule how much of the coupon must come from the *murabaha* profit, the usual minimum that is accepted is 10 per cent i.e. 10 per cent of the coupon that is being funded must be funded from the *murabaha* profit.

The *wakala* income (i.e. income from the *wakala* assets) and the *murabaha* profit will be deposited into the Collection Account.

4.4.3. Required Islamic Documentation for Sukuk-al-wakala

DOCUMENT	PARTIES	SUMMARY / PURPOSE
Wakala Agreement	Issuer SPV (as principal) and *wakeel*	This document sets out the terms of the *wakala*, the fees payable to the *wakeel*, the duration of the *wakala* and the conditions for termination. It also sets out the eligibility criteria for the assets to be selected by the *wakeel*
Asset Purchase Agreement	Seller and *wakeel*	On behalf of Issuer SPV, the *wakeel* will use the *sukuk* proceeds to purchase assets, from the Seller that comply with the eligibility criteria
Purchase Undertaking (Wa'ad)	Granted by Obligor in favour of Issuer SPV	Allows Issuer SPV to sell the *wakala* assets back to Obligor if an event of default occurs or at maturity, in return for which Obligor is required to pay (through an Exercise Price) all outstanding amounts so the Issuer SPV can pay the investors
Sale Undertaking (Wa'ad)	Granted by Issuer SPV in favour of Obligor	Allows Obligor to buy the *wakala* assets back from Issuer SPV in limited circumstances (e.g., the occurrence of a tax event), in return for which the Obligor is required to pay all outstanding amounts (through an Exercise Price) so that Issuer SPV can pay the investors
Substitution Undertaking (Wa'ad)	Granted by Obligor in favour of Issuer SPV	Issuer SPV may exercise its option to require the Obligor to purchase any of the *wakala* assets that cease to be sharia compliant in return for new sharia compliant assets or cash, which will then be used to purchase new sharia-compliant assets[4]

---

4   Alternatively, this mechanism may be achieved via the purchase undertaking.

4.4.4. Required Capital Market Documentation for Sukuk-al-wakala

DOCUMENT	PARTIES	SUMMARY / PURPOSE
Prospectus (including terms & conditions)		The Prospectus will set out key risk factors, disclosure on the Obligor and Issuer SPV as well as key other information that investors need to be aware of as part of making an informed investment decision
Declaration of Trust	Issuer SPV, Obligor and Delegate	Creation of the trust certificates and appointment of Delegate and empowering delegate to take certain actions under certain circumstances e.g. Obligor default
Agency Agreement	Issuer SPV, Obligor, Delegate, Paying Agent, Transfer Agent, Calculation Agent	Appointment of Agents
Subscription Agreement	Issuer SPV, Obligor, Joint Lead Managers	Subscription of the Sukuk by the Joint Lead Managers

4.5. Other Sukuk Structures

AAOIFI Sharia Standard No.17 (Investment Sukuk), broadly define sukuk as certificates of equal value representing undivided shares in the ownership of tangible assets, usufructs and services, or in the ownership of the assets of particular projects or special investment activities. Sukuk can therefore be interposed on any underlying sharia-compliant structure. The previous parts of this Chapter focused on those structures that are frequently implemented in the Islamic finance market. The AAOIFI Sharia Standard No. 17, however, list other types of sukuk in addition to those already discussed. A summary of some of these structures is set out below.

4.5.1. Sukuk-al-manfa'a

The *sukuk-al-manfa'a* structure envisages the grant to the Issuer SPV of a long-term right to use an asset. This grant can take a number of forms depending on the nature of the asset involved but can include, for example, an assignment or sale of certain rights in an asset to the Issuer SPV. The Issuer SPV, as owner of those rights to use, can apply those rights to use in order to generate returns for the investors. The method in which the rights to use are applied can vary depending on the nature of the asset involved and the rights to use granted to the Issuer SPV, but can include, for example, appointing a distributor for the purposes of distributing the rights to generate returns for the investors. Alternatively, the rights granted to the Issuer SPV may already be generating returns and, as owner of those rights, the Issuer SPV is entitled to receive those returns on behalf of the investors.

A number of recent structures in the airline, telecommunication and port operator industry sectors have used this structure as there is an objective methodology of being able to monitor use. So the airline sector can use ASKM/ATKM, the telecommunication sector can use minutes of airtime and the port sector can use TEU's (as the unit of measure for the pass through of container units in a port). I have been fortunate enough to lead teams involved in developing these structures and entities that have issued using ATKM include Emirates and Fly Dubai in the UAE, and Garuda in Indonesia. The TEU structure has been used by DP World in the UAE, and the airtime structure has been used by Axiata in Malaysia, Etisalat in UAE and Qtel/Ooredoo in Qatar.

4.5.2. Sukuk-al-muzara'a

A *muzara'a* contract is used in relation to sharecropping. Under a *sukuk-al-muzara'a* arrangement the Obligor would typically be an owner of land or of the usufruct of that land and the subscribers would typically be farmers (or other cultivators) who assume the obligation of cultivating the land on the basis of a *muzara'a* contract. The farmers would cultivate the land and the proceeds of the issuance would represent the costs of the cultivation. Alternatively, the Obligor can be the farmer that requires land and therefore issues *sukuk-al-muzara'a* certificates to investors. The proceeds of the issuance are then used to acquire the land for the purposes of cultivating it. In both situations, the holders of the sukuk are entitled to a share of the crop produced as a result of the cultivation. Where the investors are the farmers, the sukuk can only be traded after the crop has been produced. However, where the investors are the owners of the land, the sukuk can be traded once the sukuk have been issued and the activity on the land commences.

4.5.3. Sukuk-al-musaqa

A *musaqa* contract is similar to a *muzara'a* contract except that it is used in relation to irrigating fruit-bearing trees and spending and caring for them. Under a *sukuk-al-musaqa* arrangement the Obligor would typically be an owner of land that consists of trees or of the usufruct of that land and the subscribers would typically be workers (i.e. irrigators) who assume the obligation of irrigating the land pursuant to a *musaqa* contract. The irrigators would irrigate the trees and spend and care for them and the proceeds of the issuance would represent the costs of the irrigation and upkeep. Alternatively, the Obligor can be the irrigator and the subscribers to the sukuk can be the owners of the land. The proceeds of the issuance are then used to finance the irrigation of the land. In both situations, the holders of the sukuk are entitled to a share of the produce of the trees. Where the investors are the irrigators, the sukuk can only be traded after the produce of the trees has matured. However, where the investors are the owners of the land, the sukuk can be traded once the sukuk have been issued and the activity on the land commences.

4.5.4. Sukuk-al-mugharasa

A *mugharasa* contract is used for planting trees and undertaking the work and expenses required by such plantation. Under a *sukuk-al-mugharasa* arrangement the Obligor would typically be an owner of land suitable for planting trees and the subscribers would typically be workers (i.e. planters) who assume the obligation of planting trees on the basis of a *mugharasa* contract. The planters would plant and maintain the trees and the proceeds of the issuance would represent the costs of maintaining the plantation. Alternatively, the Obligor can be the planter and the subscribers to the sukuk can be the owners of the land. The proceeds of the issuance are then used to finance the plantation on the land. In both situations, the holders of the sukuk are entitled to a share in both the trees and the land. *Sukuk-al-mugharasa* certificates can be traded after closing of subscription and once activity on the land commences (irrespective of whether the holders of the sukuk are planters or owners of the land).

4.5.5. Sukuk-al-salam

Generally, in order for a sale to be valid under sharia the object forming the subject matter of the sale must be in existence and in the physical or constructive possession of the seller. The exceptions to this general position are sales effected pursuant to *salam* and *istisna* contracts.

In its simplest form, a *salam* contract involves the purchase of assets by one party from another party on immediate payment and deferred delivery terms. The purchase price of the assets is typically referred to as the *salam* capital and is paid at the time of entering into the *salam* contract. The assets sold under the *salam* contract are referred to as *al-mu'salam fihi*, delivery of which is deferred until a future date.

A *salam* contract may be construed as being synonymous with the objective of a forward sale contract. Forward sale contracts are generally forbidden under sharia unless the element of uncertainty (*gharar*) inherent in such contracts is effectively eradicated. For this reason, certain criteria must be met in order for a *salam* contract to be sharia compliant.

Although the use of *salam* has been, and is, utilised by some institutions for short-term liquidity purposes, its use as the platform for issuing sukuk, as an alternative to conventional bonds, is rare in comparison to some of the more prevalent structures like *sukuk-al-ijara*. The limited use of this structure can be attributed to a number of factors, namely the non-tradability of the sukuk and the requirement that the Obligor must be able to deliver certain 'standardised' assets to the Issuer SPV at certain future dates which may be difficult where the Obligor's business model does not provide for this.

4.5.6. Sukuk-al-istisna

Alternatively referred to as the 'Islamic project bond', the structure of *sukuk-al-istisna* has not been that widely used. Although, at first glance, the structure appears ideal for the financing of greenfield development, certain structural drawbacks have proven difficult to overcome and, as a result, *sukuk-al-istisna* has not featured as an alternative source of Islamic funding on multi-sourced project financing in the manner once predicted.

Of particular significance is the prevailing view that *sukuk-al-istisna* are not tradable during the construction period. In addition to this, the different approaches taken by sharia scholars to advance rentals and *istisna* termination payments have also led structurers to consider other more 'flexible' structures (such as *sukuk-al-musharaka*).

Broadly speaking, *istisna* translates as being 'to order a manufacturer to manufacture a specific good for the purchaser'. Under an *istisna*, it is important that the price and specification of the good to be manufactured are agreed at the outset.

In the modern-day context of Islamic finance, the *istisna* has developed into a particularly useful tool in the Islamic funding of the construction phase of a project – it is often regarded as being similar to a fixed-price 'turnkey' contract.

In order to enable investors to receive a return during the period where assets are being constructed under an *istisna* arrangement, some sharia scholars have permitted the use of a forward lease arrangement (known as *ijara mawsufah fi al-dimmah*) alongside such *istisna* arrangement. Accordingly, *sukuk-al-istisna* often combines an *istisna* arrangement with a forward lease arrangement – whilst the *istisna* is the method through which the investors can advance funds to an Obligor, the *ijara* provides the most compatible payment method to those investors.

The use of staged payments (a common feature in *istisna* construction arrangements – see further below) may however result in an unutilised amount of sukuk proceeds being held in the structure for a prolonged period during construction (pending the achievement of the relevant milestones). Accordingly, it may be necessary to consider investing these amounts in sharia-compliant investments in order to mitigate negative carry (i.e. periodic distributions continue to be payable whilst cash remains unutilised – a position which is likely to be unacceptable to the Obligor).

CHAPTER 5

SUKUK AND THE MODERN FINANCIAL SYSTEM INFRASTRUCTURE

IT IS IMPORTANT to understand the architecture of the financial system for fixed-income securities as sukuk instruments also utilise this same infrastructure, particularly so for the purposes of settlement, trading and redemption.

There is a difference in the architecture used for what is referred to as 'Regulation S' sukuk and '144a' sukuk. Generally speaking, a Regulation S sukuk can be marketed and sold to investors outside the US only, whereas a 144a sukuk can be marketed and sold to investors in the US.

The distinction between a Regulation S sukuk and a 144a sukuk has no impact on the Islamic structure that may be used to structure a sukuk or the commercial intention behind issuing the sukuk. From a high-level perspective, it only impacts the level of financial disclosure required by the Obligor, the level of auditors' comfort provided to the lead managers on the financial information in the prospectus, and the type of entity that may be authorised to market/sell the sukuk to investors in the US.

I will now explore the architecture of a Regulation S sukuk in detail:

5.1. Registered Sukuk vs Bearer Sukuk

Most sukuk traded in the international debt capital markets are, conceptually, global instruments where the Registrar will maintain the list of registered noteholders. For a bearer sukuk, the title passes on physical delivery, rather than on annotation on a register. Bearer instruments are largely no longer used due to a combination of tax reasons and the high level of compliance associated with it.

5.2. Definitive Sukuk certificate vs Global Sukuk Certificate

A sukuk can be issued in global form or in definitive form (the same way as a conventional bond).

A 'definitive' certificate means that each underlying investor will receive a certificate for itself, either in physical form or in electronic form. The Issuer SPV will issue multiple definitive certificates which when aggregated add up to the total amount of the issuance. A 'global' certificate means that an issued single document represents the entire sukuk with the terms and conditions attached. There is only a single 'certificate' issued on the issuance date of the sukuk in the name of the 'common safekeeper' for a new global note and in the name of the 'common depositary' for the classic global note.

New global note (NGN) and classic global note (CGN) are two different types of global sukuk certificates.

5.2.1. New Global Note (NGN)

As NGN requires the Obligor and an International Central Securities Depositary (ICSD) to have entered into an Issuer-ICSD Agreement.

The Obligor will appoint a commercial bank – under a paying agency agreement – to act as its Paying Agent, which will also act as a 'common safekeeper' (CSK) and a 'common service provider' (CSP). Each are appointed by the ICSD and act as an agent on behalf of the ICSD. The CSK provides safekeeping services for the ICSD and the CSP provides asset services to the ICSD.

So the commercial bank has three roles: (i) Paying Agent of the Obligor; (ii) CSK for the ICSD; and (iii) CSP for the ICSD.

The steps for an NGN are:

- Delivery of the NGN by the Issuer SPV/Obligor to the CSK. The registered owner of the NGN is a nominee of the CSK.
- Issuer-ICSD Agreement, which must be signed by the Obligor prior to the acceptance of the NGN by the ICSD (or the CSK as an agent of the ICSD).

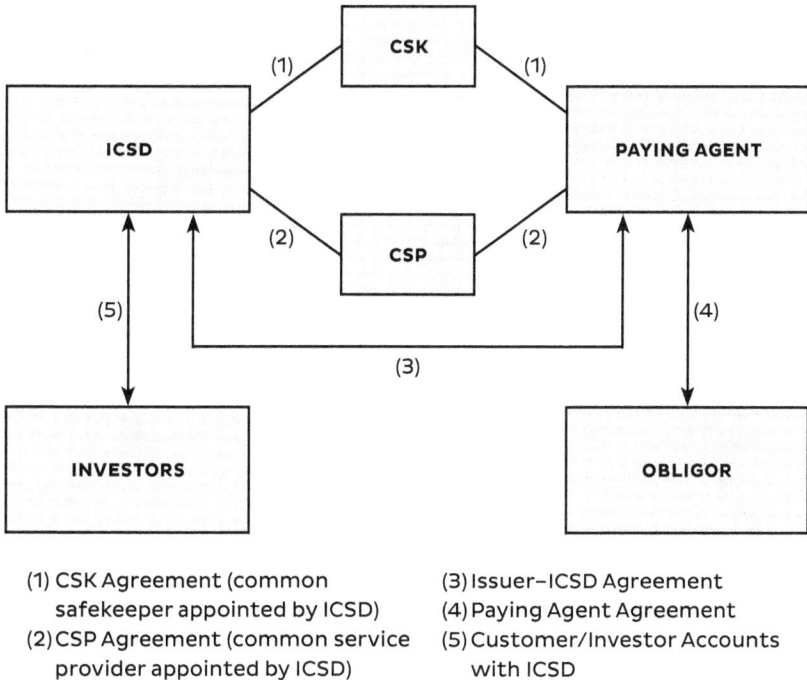

(1) CSK Agreement (common safekeeper appointed by ICSD)
(2) CSP Agreement (common service provider appointed by ICSD)
(3) Issuer–ICSD Agreement
(4) Paying Agent Agreement
(5) Customer/Investor Accounts with ICSD

Figure 5.2.1: A diagrammatic representation of the NGN parties

- Effectuation Instruction and Disposal Authority, which allows the CSK to sign the NGN and make it a valid security.
- CSK Election Form, which is sent by the Paying Agent and for depositing NGN with the ICSD as CSK.

The key difference between NGN and CGN is that for NGNs, the ICSD's records, rather than physical annotations on the global note itself, are used to determine the sukuk's outstanding amount.

5.2.2. Classic Global Note

A CGN does not require the Obligor and the ICSD to have entered into an Issuer-ICSD Agreement but uses a deposit structure where the global note is deposited with the bank that is acting as the common depositary.

The common depositary acts on behalf of the ICSD (the most common one for Reg S sukuk being Euroclear/Clearstream) and will be the legal owner of the global note.

The Obligor will appoint a commercial bank to act as its Paying Agent under a paying agency agreement and this bank will also act as the common depositary.

The process is as follows:
- The Issuer SPV will instruct the Registrar to authenticate the global note (or authenticate in accordance with the paying agency agreement) and deliver it to the common depositary.
- The Registrar will confirm that the global note has been registered in the name of the common depositary (or its nominee).
- The Issuer SPV will send an instruction letter to the common depositary instructing the common depositary to hold the global note on behalf of Issuer SPV until such time as the Lead Manager has provided payment instructions for the issuance

proceeds to be transferred to the Obligor. At that point, the common depositary holds the global note on behalf of the ICSD (which in turn acts on behalf of the investors/subscribers).

- The Issuer SPV will send a letter of instruction to the Settlement Lead Manager to instruct it to make payment of the issuance amount (in discharge of the Lead Managers' obligation to pay for the certificates under the placement/subscription agreement) to the account of the Obligor.

- The Settlement Lead Manager will send a letter of authorisation (on behalf of all the Lead Managers) instructing the common depositary to hold the global certificate (settled free of payment) for the account of the ICSD (which in turn acts for the account of the investors).

- The common depositary will send an acknowledgement confirming that it holds the global note on behalf of the ICSD (which in turn acts for the accounts of the Investors.)

- Finally, the Obligor sends an acknowledgement of funds received, in satisfaction of the Issuer SPV's obligation to pay the consideration under the relevant Islamic document.

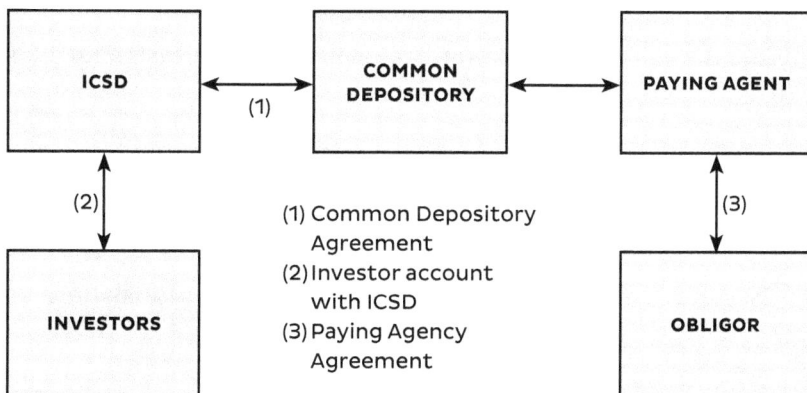

Figure 5.2.2: A diagrammatic representation of the CGN parties

In the CGN, it is physical annotations on the global note itself by the common depositary that are used to determine the outstanding amount of the issue.

Therefore when a sukuk is issued in classic global form, the common depositary (or its nominee) is the registered holder of the sukuk, and all payments of profit and principal are made to the common depositary as the registered holder of the global sukuk. The common depositary holds the global note on behalf of the ICSD, which acts on behalf of the investors. So, when the ICSD receives the funds, it passes them on to underlying investors by crediting their cash account with the ICSD.

Trading in sukuk is over-the-counter and occurs through the crediting and debiting of securities and cash accounts held with the relevant clearing systems (such as Euroclear and Clearstream in the Eurobond market), and investors in bonds often hold their investment through complex chains of contractual relationships with custodians (or intermediaries), culminating with an 'accountholder' – a financial institution which holds a securities and cash account with the clearing system.

Putting this into the context of an individual sukuk investor, such an investor will therefore have an indirect interest in the sukuk assets through a complicated financial infrastructure as follows:

First, the Issuer SPV will declare a trust in favour of the direct sukuk holder, which will be the registered owner of the global note i.e. the common depositary.

Second, the common depositary holds the global note as agent/trustee of the clearing system.

Third, the clearing system will hold its ownership interest in the global note on behalf of each individual investor that has contributed funds to the purchase of that note. That ownership interest of each individual is evidenced by the clearing system crediting the respective securities account of the individual investors.

Fourth, only institutional investors – and not retail investors – are permitted to open securities accounts with the clearing system. Retail investors will therefore usually appoint an institutional investor to hold a portion of the global note on its behalf. So, an ultimate sukuk investor does have a beneficial right to the sukuk assets but this is through a complex architectural arrangement.

Bringing this all together, let's take the example of Obligor issuing *sukuk-al-ijara* certificates worth USD 100 million, and look at the various procedural steps from a timeline perspective. For this example, I have assumed a sovereign issuer so there is no requirement for the involvement of an auditor, financial statements or an auditor engagement or comfort letter.

The following points will discuss the action that is required based on a timeline starting from the signing date of the subscription agreement:

- **Pre-announcement** - All transaction documents agreed (including all Islamic documents and all capital market documents) between the Obligor, Issuer SPV, Lead Managers and all third parties including the Delegate/Paying Agent/clearing systems. For a *sukuk-al-ijara* this will include the following:
  - Capital Market documents: Prospectus, Declaration of Trust, (Paying) Agency Agreement, Subscription Agreement.
  - Islamic documents: Sale and purchase agreement, *ijara* agreement, service agency agreement, purchase undertaking and sale undertaking.

The draft prospectus is approved by the relevant stock exchange and/or listing authority (which results in a 'preliminary' offering circular or 'red'). The 'red' does not include any pricing information or issuance amount as this is yet to be confirmed.

Draft fatwa is made available i.e. sharia scholars sign-off on transaction documents.

- **Announcement** - Announcement of the proposed transaction and the commencement of the marketing phase. Immediately prior to the commence of the announcement there is a pre-announcement bring down diligence. This is basically the Obligor confirming that the information in the 'red' remains true and correct and this is required to ensure the lead managers are not marketing any transaction where the prospectus is misleading in any way. Lead Managers/Obligor will be marketing to potential investors (note that marketing of fixed income securities such as sukuk is a regulated activity and marketing can only be done on the basis of appropriate licenses and regulatory approvals).[5]

- **Marketing Phase** - The marketing phase can be very short (e.g. even less than one day) if the Obligor is a regular and frequent issuer in the capital markets, or can be slightly longer (e.g. 2 or 3 days). The key is that the lead managers/Obligors are speaking to all key investors.

- **Bookbuilding** - The end of the marketing phase is marked by the book-building process. At the end of the marketing phase the lead

---

5 For example, marketing into Saudi Arabia requires the draft prospectus to have been filed with the Saudi CMA at least 10 clear days before marketing begins. Marketing into Malaysia require the draft prospectus to have been filed with the Malaysian Securities Commission before marketing begins, with confirmation of which Lead Managers have issued a fatwa for the transaction.

managers will have a sense of the proposed level of interest and will then announce a transaction to the market with an indicative issuance amount (i.e. USD 100 million) and indicative pricing. Investors will then submit their orders to the Lead Managers/Bookrunners and this will then allow the Lead Managers to finalise issuance amount and pricing based on investor demand.

- **Pricing** - The book building phase ends with a confirmation of the commercial elements of the issuance, namely the size of the issuance and the pricing. Orders from investors are confirmed on the basis of the final pricing. The LEI for each of the Obligor and the Issuer SPV must be in place no later than that time of pricing.[6] In addition the ISIN is made available once the term sheet is finalised.[7] Each issuance has its own ISIN so if the same Issuer SPV has issued multiple series on a programme, the Issuer SPV will have one LEI but each issuance/series will have its own ISIN.

- **Signing** - Signing will typically happen two days after pricing (and this allows time for each lead manager to finalise arrangements between itself and prospective investors). Signing of the Subscription Agreement occurs between the Obligor, Issuer SPV and the Lead Managers and the subscription agreement is effective. At this point the Lead Managers are legally committing to subscribe for the sukuk certificates being issued by the Issuer SPV by signing the subscription agreement.

---

6   LEI is the Legal Entity Identifier is a 20-character code that is based on the ISO 17442 standard developed by the International Organisation for Standardisation (ISO). LEI number is used as a reference for important information that offers transparency when taking part in financial transactions such as sukuk.

7   ISIN is the International Securities Identification Number and is a unique number for each issuance.

- **Closing** - Closing happens on a T+3 or T+5 basis i.e. 3 or 5 days after the signing date. On the closing date:
  - The Declaration of Trust/Paying Agency Agreement are signed, dated and effective and the global note/sukuk is created.
  - The Islamic documents are signed and dated (for an *ijara* transaction this would be the sale agreement, *ijara* agreement, service agency agreement, purchase undertaking and sale undertaking). The sale of the sukuk assets to the Issuer is completed and the lease/ijara to the Obligor is effective.
  - The global certificate is authenticated by the Registrar and delivered to the common depositary. The various confirmations and instructions are sent by the common depositary and lead managers (as set out earlier in this Chapter 5, *Sukuk and the Modern Financial System Infrastructure*) and the issuance proceeds of USD 100 million are released to the Obligor.
  - The legal opinions by legal counsel to the Obligor, Issuer SPV and Lead Managers are issued. The final fatwa (i.e. sharia pronouncement) is issued by the relevant sharia scholars/board.
  - The final prospectus (referred to as the 'black') which includes the issuance size and the pricing is submitted to the exchange for final approval and sukuk certificates are admitted to listing.

CHAPTER 6

RECENT DEVELOPMENTS

AS MENTIONED in Chapter 1, the Higher Sharia Authority (the HSA) in the UAE has now mandated the application of AAOIFI standards on all new sukuk transactions where a UAE-based Islamic bank or conventional bank that offers Islamic finance services is involved (either as Obligor or Lead Manager).

Whilst new sharia standards are continuously being added each year by the AAOIFI, certain standards have been in existence for several years. Whilst they may not have historically been fully applied in the UAE, that is now no longer the case. Some of the key developments in the last 12 months include AAOIFI Standard No. 59, issued in 2019 and mandated for use for all sukuk from 2020.

There are a number of important requirements as a result of AAOIFI Standard No. 59, which impact all sukuk transactions. The key points include:

- A sukuk structured on a *murabaha*-basis only (i.e. *sukuk-al-murabaha*) is no longer permitted. Whilst this is still used for domestic transactions in certain countries such as Malaysia, it is no longer possible for a standalone structure in the UAE.

- A sukuk must have a minimum tangibility of 51 per cent. If the sukuk tangibility drops below this level, certain remedial steps must be taken by the Obligor. However, if the tangibility drops below 33 per cent, then steps must be taken to prevent any secondary market trading of the sukuk, including delisting the sukuk in the event it is listed on a stock exchange. As certain fixed-income investors are only able to hold listed securities, this delisting event is coupled with the right of an investor to redeem the sukuk in the event of a delisting. In certain deals, the occurrence of a tangibility event is built into the concept of the dissolution events, so a breach of the tangibility ratio will trigger a dissolution of the sukuk; however, with the latter, it is worth noting that this will also trigger cross-default on other bonds/sukuk issued by the same Obligor.

- Intangible receivables can no longer be used as the basis for structuring sukuk. An Islamic bank will have made retail and corporate Islamic loans to customers/clients using the *murabaha* mode of financing. Historically, an Islamic bank that may have wanted to issue a sukuk would have used these *murabaha* financial assets, which are receivables only, as part of the sukuk assets. This is no longer permitted. Additionally, the use of other intangible assets such as *istisna* assets during construction are also not permitted.

- Whilst the use of a *murabaha* component in a *wakala* sukuk is still permitted[8] (provided the overall tangibility ratio is not

---

8   The Issuer SPV will use part of the issuance proceeds to buy commodities and then on-sell them to the Obligor for a deferred payment price. This is different from where the Obligor has *murabaha* receivables on its balance sheet and sells these to the Issuer SPV. For further details, please see *sukuk-al-wakala* set out in Chapter 4, Part 4.4.

breached), the *murabaha* portion of the sukuk cannot be structured on the basis of a floating profit rate. The profit rate on
the *murabaha* must be fixed. This introduces more complexity
for floating rate sukuk and as a result, floating rate mechanics
have essentially been removed from the vast majority of sukuk
transactions.

In addition to AAOIFI Standard No. 59, the applicability of
AAOIFI Sharia Standards, in general, has resulted in a number of
refinements to established structures and documents, including,
as follows:

• Service Agency mechanics – as mentioned in Part 4.2 (*Sukuk-
al-ijara*), the Issuer SPV and Obligor enter into a service agency
agreement whereby Issuer SPV will appoint Obligor as its
Servicing Agent to carry out certain of its obligations under
the lease arrangement, namely the obligation to undertake any
major maintenance, insurance (or *takaful*) and payment of taxes
in connection with the Sukuk Assets. The traditional position
used to be that to the extent that Obligor (as Servicing Agent)
claims any costs and expenses for performing these obligations
(the Servicing Costs), the rental for the subsequent lease period
under the lease arrangement will be increased by an equivalent
amount (a Supplemental Rental). This Supplemental Rental due
from Obligor (as Lessee) will be set off against the obligation of
Trustee to pay the Servicing Costs. However, this position has
now evolved driven by sharia concerns that it is unconsidered
unfair to contractually demand that the Obligor (in its capacity) as lessee be obliged to pay Supplementary Rent simply
because the Obligor (in its capacity as Servicing Agent) has
claimed Servicing Costs. Whilst the economics of the sukuk

remain the same – given the commercial intention is to have a senior unsecured fixed income instrument – the methodology and approach has changed so that the Servicing Agent is provided funds to perform such servicing/maintenance at the time of issuance from the issuance proceeds. So rather than 100 per cent of the issuance proceeds being used to pay for the sale of the *ijara* assets, the SPV Trustee may use a lower amount, e.g. 95 per cent to fund the purchase of the *ijara* assets and the balance of the issuance proceeds (e.g. 5 per cent) is granted to the Obligor as a pre-funding of the service agency costs that may be incurred.

• Previously, the accepted position was that a partial loss of the lease assets would have no impact on the sukuk (i.e. the lessee would be obliged to continue to pay rent in full) so the Issuer SPV would continue to pay coupon in full to Investors. However, the current position in the UAE is that upon a partial loss, the lessee must: (i) have the right to request a refund of rent for the period of time the lease continues with the partially destroyed lease assets (the Rent Refund); and (ii) have the right to request the termination of the lease. To ensure that, from an Investors perspective, there is no reduction in the amount of coupon/periodic distribution amount as a result of a Rent Refund, the Obligor is now required to maintain insurance for any Rent Refund that may arise as a result of a partial loss, in addition to insurance for total loss (the Rent Refund Insurance Amount). So, to the extent there is a partial loss, and the lessee demands a Rent Refund, then the aggregate of: (i) the reduced rent received by the Issuer SPV from the Obligor lessee; and (ii) the Rent Refund Insurance Amount received by the Issuer SPV from the Obligor as servicing agent, will be equal to the periodic distribution amount due. The lessee will now also have the right to request a termination of the lease upon the occurrence of a partial loss, and this will now be an early dissolution event similar to the occurrence of a total loss.

- Purchase undertaking indemnity – the purchase undertaking contains an obligation of the Obligor to pay an amount required to redeem the Sukuk, and this amount is payable by the Obligor to the SPV Trustee as consideration for the purchase of the sukuk assets. So, for example, on a *sukuk-al-ijara* this amount payable by the Obligor is referred to as the 'Exercise Price'. In the event the Obligor (or a liquidator) challenges the obligation of the Obligor to pay this 'Exercise Price', then there is a fall-back indemnity on the Obligor to indemnify the SPV Trustee for an amount equal to the Exercise Price. Whereas, previously, there was no discussion around the sharia efficacy of the indemnity payment, the new HSA position is that it must be clear that any indemnity payment made by the Obligor is in exchange for either the transfer of the sukuk assets (whatever the nature of that interest may be) to the Obligor, or in exchange for the Issuer SPV relinquishing any rights it may have in the sukuk assets.
- Sharia Adviser appointment – requirement to appoint a sharia advisor for the issuance.

OVERVIEW OF KEY PRINCIPLES OF ISLAMIC FINANCE

HERE ARE SOME of the key sharia principles underlying the various Islamic finance structures:

Interest (referred to as *riba*)

The main principle and the one most people have heard of it the prohibition on interest. Under sharia principles, money is regarded as having no intrinsic value and also no time valueit is seen merely as a means of exchange. Islamic principles require that any return on funds provided by the financiers be earned by way of profit derived from a commercial risk taken by the financiers. The payment and receipt of interest (*riba*) under Islamic law is prohibited and any obligation to pay interest is considered void. Therefore all Islamic finance structures will involve the use of an asset either to buy/sell/lease/construct etc.

For the academic readers, you may be interested to know that in Islamic finance jurisprudence there are two forms of *riba* – the first, referred to as *riba al-nasiya* is interest or return on capital. The second form is referred to as *riba al-fadl* which is the exchange of unequal quantities or qualities of a commotiy. When we refer to *riba* in the context of 'interest', we refer to *riba al-nasiya*.

Speculation (referred to as *maisir*)

Contracts which involve speculation are not permissible (*haram*) and are considered void. Islamic law does not, however, prohibit general commercial speculation (which is evident in most commercial transactions). The concern is to prohibit forms of speculation which are regarded as akin to gambling. The test is whether something has been gained by chance, rather than by productive effort.

Unjust enrichment/Unfair exploitation

Contracts where one party is regarded as having unjustly gained at the expense of another are considered void under Islamic law. The sharia principle of unjust enrichment is wide in its scope; whilst it applies to an enrichment of one party at the expense of another which cannot be justified, it also extends to the enrichment of one party who exercises undue influence or duress over another. For example, it is not possible for a creditor to benefit financially from penalising a non-performing or defaulting debtor by charging and retaining a default fee. It is, however, usually permitted to charge a late payment fee or request a donation and pay the proceeds of that fee/donation to charity, since it is considered that the obligation to pay this late payment fee or donaiton would serve to encourage the debtor to discharge its contractual obligations in a timely manner.

Uncertainty (referred to as *gharrar*)

Contracts which contain uncertainty (*gharrar*), particularly any uncertainty as to one of the fundamental terms of the contract (such as the subject matter, price or time for delivery), are again considered void under Islamic law. The Islamic principle of *gharrar* is wide as it requires absolute certainty on all fundamental terms. In addition, sharia does not permit a contract where uncertainty may arise out of the actual subject matter or substance of a contract. For example, a conventional insurance arrangement is not permissible on the basis of, amongst other things, uncertainty (*gharrar*); it being uncertain whether the insured event will occur.

Unethical investments

Proceeds raised through Islamic financing cannot be used for the purposes of purchasing or investing in products that are prohibited under sharia. These include investments into sectors or companies which have as their primary business alcohol, pornography, gambling and firearms.

There is also a requirement to look at the financial ratios of companies in determining whether they are ethical or not – even if a company operates in a sharia compliant sector (e.g. food sector) the company will still be considered unethical if it highly leveraged (i.e. the amount of conventional debt it has relative to its assets is excessive). Key financial ratios which are looked at include leverage, interest income from investments and cash on deposit.

www.ingramcontent.com/pod-product-compliance
Lightning Source LLC
Chambersburg PA
CBHW061259220326
41599CB00028B/5712